MW01506242

GRASS
ISN'T
GREENER

GRASS *ISN'T* GREENER

- -

The Everyday Conservationist's Guide
to Bringing Nature to Your Yard

DANAE WOLFE

Timber Press · Portland, OR

To my husband, whose steadfast support has been the fertile soil in which this book grew. Thank you for creating a home and a haven where creativity and conservation thrive.

And to my children who have grown alongside our garden. May this book serve as a reminder that you can make a difference in the world.

Copyright © 2025 by Danae Wolfe. All rights reserved. Photo and illustration credits appear on page 228.

Hachette Book Group supports the right to free expression and the value of copyright. The purpose of copyright is to encourage writers and artists to produce the creative works that enrich our culture. The scanning, uploading, and distribution of this book without permission is a theft of the author's intellectual property. If you would like permission to use material from the book (other than for review purposes), please contact permissions@hbgusa.com. Thank you for your support of the author's rights.

Timber Press
Workman Publishing
Hachette Book Group, Inc.
1290 Avenue of the Americas
New York, New York 10104
timberpress.com

Timber Press is an imprint of Workman Publishing, a division of Hachette Book Group, Inc. The Timber Press name and logo are registered trademarks of Hachette Book Group, Inc.

Printed in China on responsibly sourced paper

Text and cover design by Hillary Caudle

The publisher is not responsible for websites (or their content) that are not owned by the publisher.

The Hachette Speakers Bureau provides a wide range of authors for speaking events. To find out more, go to hachettespeakersbureau.com or email hachettespeakers-ers@hbgusa.com.

ISBN 978-1-64326-329-8

A catalog record for this book is available from the Library of Congress.

Contents

Preface

As I set out to write this book, I had the great fortune of visiting a diversity of wildlife gardens and landscapes that seamlessly blend home with habitat. One thing I found particularly striking during these visits was that I was almost always met with an apology. From the most tediously tended landscapes to the wilder spaces that blurred the boundary between garden and ecosystem, homeowners felt compelled to share all the ways their gardens weren't good enough.

"I'm sorry it's not mulched."

"I should have weeded before you came."

"I hope it's okay that not everything in my garden is native."

And yet, each of these gardens shared one thing in common—a gardener who was willing to take that first step toward stewarding a different kind of landscape, one that embraces the idea that each of us holds the power to ignite change.

We've created ecological imbalance in our pursuit of a garden aesthetic. But how might our gardens look and function differently if we instead viewed them through the lens of supporting wildlife and building ecological function, rather than through the lens of form and beauty that appeals only to us humans? What if we celebrated our gardens as an oasis of shelter and sustenance for wildlife who have called this land home for millennia instead of lamenting over holes in leaves and nibbled blooms? What if we came to understand that creating spaces that support wildlife simultaneously provides a multitude of benefits for people too?

Change is possible. And it starts here. Conservation is not reserved for some special group with whom the responsibility has been bestowed. Conservation starts at home. It begins in backyards and on balconies. It thrives in community gardens and in local parks and nature preserves. And it endures in every act—both big and small—that considers the bees and the butterflies, the turtles and the toads, the bats and the birds.

By exploring the practices in this book, I hope that you will feel emboldened to take that first step toward creating a more equitable and sustainable relationship with nature, a relationship built not on extraction but on stewardship. Saving the planet is the biggest and most important group project of our lives. By practicing homegrown conservation, I hope you will begin to see your role shift from landscape manager to steward of Earth and all its creatures. But remember this: while change is desperately needed, it won't happen overnight. Give yourself grace as you learn and grow and garden.

Introduction:

ECOLOGY IN THE ANTHROPO- CENE

Look outside. Whether you live in a city or suburb, on a farm or on the coast, the world around you is likely scarred by the imprint of humans. The climate is warming. Forests are burning. Oceans are rising. Habitats are dwindling and those that remain are overrun with invasive species. And wildlife has been hunted to extirpation and extinction. Colonization of land throughout the last few centuries, marked by explosive population growth, has created an impact on the Earth unmatched by any other time in history. This is the Anthropocene, the current geological age defined by how human activity has transformed the planet's climate and ecosystems.

Warm Is the New Norm

Temperatures on Earth have been in flux since the birth of the planet 4.5 billion years ago, but never in the last 10,000 years have temperatures changed so rapidly than in the most recent century and a half. Driven by increased atmospheric carbon due largely to human activities, Earth's mean temperatures have increased around two degrees Fahrenheit (or one degree Celsius) since the late 19th century. While two degrees might not seem huge, this increase in temperature is wreaking havoc on the planet and its people.

Climate change is causing glaciers to melt at an unprecedented rate, diverting fresh water into the world's oceans, which causes sea levels to rise and puts millions of people at risk of severe flood events and coastal erosion. The frequency and intensity of severe storms is also increasing, leading to periods of heavier rainfall and more destructive tropical storms during the rainy season and more intense periods of drought during the dry season, which increase the likelihood of catastrophic wildfires. And ocean acidification is accelerating, making it more difficult for calcium-dependent organisms like corals and mollusks to build and maintain their calcium carbonate shells and skeletons, creating impacts that ripple throughout our oceans.

Biodiversity at Risk

From bacteria and fungi to plants and wildlife, every living thing has a role to play within its native ecosystem. Soil is teeming with a diversity of microorganisms, which help to maintain the integrity of healthy plant communities the world over. Insects and other arthropods help pollinate plants, decompose dead and decaying organic matter, and sustain essential predator-prey relationships in ecosystems everywhere. Herbivores consume massive volumes of plants each day and redistribute nutrients and energy

CLIMATE CHANGE

Climate change refers to the long-term alteration of Earth's average temperatures and weather patterns. Since the 1800s, climate change has been primarily driven by human activities, including the burning of fossil fuels, deforestation, and industrialization, all of which release greenhouse gases like carbon dioxide and methane into the atmosphere. These gases trap heat from the sun and lead to a gradual warming of the planet, creating far-reaching consequences for nearly all life on Earth.

throughout food chains as they are subsequently eaten by predators. Trees throughout the world's forests absorb billions of metric tons of carbon dioxide each year while providing oxygen for life on Earth. And reefs and mangroves form protective barriers that help slow the movement of waves hitting coastlines, protecting coastal communities from erosion.

Every living thing and the habitats they need to thrive are woven together in a grand tapestry of life on Earth. Pulling just one thread is enough to unravel it all. And yet, all around us, threads are being tugged and torn. Climate change; habitat destruction and fragmentation; conversion of land for agriculture, urbanization and development; invasive species; overconsumption and exploitation of resources; and pollution are threatening the world's biodiversity.

Biodiversity, which refers to the variety of life in the world or in a particular habitat, fosters ecosystem stability, resilience, and productivity. It also supports essential ecosystem services like pollination, purification of air and water, erosion and flood control, carbon sequestration, and climate regulation. In many ways, a biodiverse ecosystem is like a well-stocked toolbox: if you break or lose one tool, you have many others that can help get the job done. But having only a hammer won't suffice when you're building an entire house. Just as a well-equipped toolbox provides backup options for various tasks, a diverse ecosystem with many species ensures that vital ecological functions can continue even if disturbance or the loss of a species impacts part of the system. But with each passing year, we lose more tools in our toolbox.

Plants are disappearing at an alarming rate, with some scientists estimating that the rate of

FROM LEFT
Healthy forests absorb billions of metric tons of carbon dioxide each year.

Amur honeysuckle, a common invasive shrub in North America, spreads aggressively, outcompetes native plants, and threatens wildlife habitat.

CLOCKWISE
Decline of wild blue lupine
has resulted in the decline
of the specialist species
that depend on the plant
for survival, like the fed-
erally endangered Karner
blue butterfly.

Due to commercial hunt-
ing and habitat modifica-
tion, beaver populations
in North America dropped
to near extinction by the
mid-1800s.

Monarch butterflies were
added to the IUCN's Red
List of threatened species
in 2022.

The introduction of
non-native and invasive
species, like this Chinese
praying mantis, disrupts
ecosystems and may lead
to increased predation of
vulnerable species.

plant extinction is up to 500 times faster today than what would be expected to naturally occur if not for human factors, putting as much as 40 percent of the world's plant species at risk of extinction (Humphreys et al., 2019). The outlook for mammals is equally dim. Around 27 percent of wild mammals are threatened, and looking at the distributed biomass of mammals in the world, it's no wonder why. Wild mammals make up just three percent of mammalian biomass on the planet, with humans and livestock accounting for 35 percent and 62 percent respectively, no doubt a sign of the western world's firm grip on meat-heavy diets (Greenspoon et al., 2023). Sadly, plants and mammals aren't the only ones at risk.

With nearly one million described species and millions more yet to be discovered, insects are the largest and most abundant group of animals. From bees and butterflies to beetles and ants, insects provide ecosystem services unmatched by other animal groups. Unfortunately, insects around the world are dwindling. Around 40 percent of insect species are in decline and one third are endangered (Sánchez-Bayo & Wyckhuys, 2019). Because insects create important links in nearly all food webs on Earth, the loss of these six-legged animals has devastating impacts for wildlife everywhere, including the birds, reptiles, and amphibians that depend on them for survival.

According to the International Union for Conservation of Nature (IUCN), more than 42,100 species are threatened with extinction, including 41 percent of assessed amphibian species, 21 percent of assessed reptile species, and 13 percent of assessed bird species. Climate change has packed a particularly bad punch for life beneath the sea, with one report noting that marine wildlife has declined nearly 50 percent since 1970. Species that are used for human consumption have fared even worse, with estimates suggesting we've lost as much as 74 percent of tuna and mackerel in our oceans due to overfishing.

Unfortunately, the impacts of environmental issues are not confined to wildlife alone. In many areas of the world, socioeconomically disadvantaged communities are disproportionately impacted by climate-related events due to lack of resources that allow them to adapt and recover from environmental disasters, such as hurricanes, floods, and wildfires. Insufficient infrastructure, inadequate housing, and lack of financial resources make it difficult for residents to prepare for, respond to, and rebuild after such events, leaving them even more vulnerable to the long-term consequences of climate change. Simply put, climate change is as much a people issue as it is a nature issue.

Gray tree frog

A Call for Help

The good news is, we started with the bad news. If this grim outlook has you feeling down, know this: by creating climate- and wildlife-friendly home landscapes, you can bolster biodiversity while reducing the impacts of climate change in your own community. Rest assured we're not talking about returning Earth to the way it was before humans began to radically alter the landscape—we simply cannot revert to some previously saved version of the planet as if it were a computer file. Conservation and restoration are not so easy. In fact, understanding the best approach to conservation—especially in a rapidly changing world—is quite complicated. Scientists and researchers are working every day to address the twin crises of climate change and biodiversity loss. But closer to home, there is work to be done too.

We may never return Earth to a version unaltered by people—and we shouldn't have to. People are part of nature. We've altered the landscape in unimaginable ways, we've left deep imprints on most parts of this Earth, and we've created systems based on consumerism and extraction. But we are nature, and we are not the sole species to create such everlasting change on the land. As the dominant species, however, we have not only an opportunity but the responsibility to steward Earth and its creatures with care, to find balance in how we live upon the planet, and to move from extractive to regenerative systems that support both people and wildlife. And we can start in our own gardens.

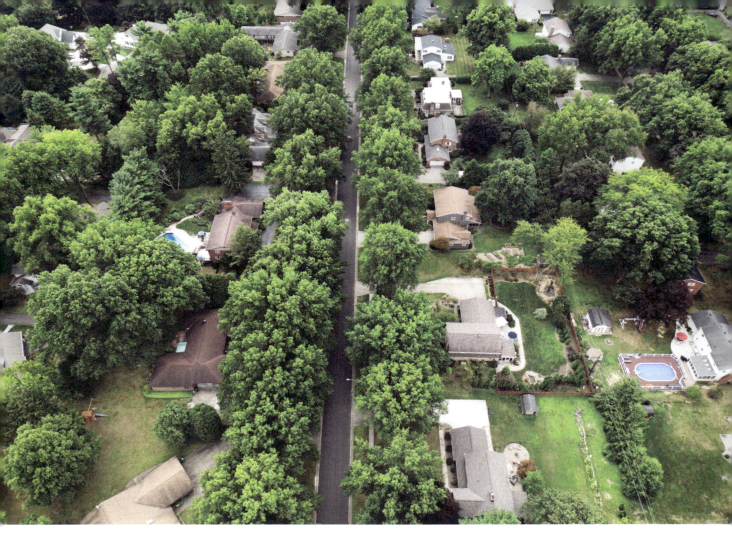

Planting native plants in our home landscapes is a great way to start restoring ecosystem function to our communities.

Chapter 1

UNDER-STAND YOUR LAND

When it comes to gardening for wildlife, the dominant narrative has largely focused on restoring native plants to the landscape. Planting native is essential, yes. But creating an oasis for nature and wildlife requires a more holistic approach, one that considers the bigger picture of your landscape. You might be tempted to run out and purchase every beautiful native bloom that you see at your local garden center, promising yourself or your partner that you'll find a spot for it. But it's a good idea to have a plan before jumping in with both feet. Creating that plan will require a basic understanding of what you're working with.

Survey Your Space

The traditional home landscape is a place of control. We've tamed these spaces to make them more comfortable and accommodating for us. In doing so, we've made them uncomfortable and unaccommodating for most anything else. Plants are placed neatly in rows behind perfectly edged borders. Lush green lawns greet visitors and passersby. Leaves and dead stems are swiftly removed from garden beds. And poisons are poured generously throughout to ensure that the undesirables don't make themselves too comfortable.

For centuries, gardeners have sought to bend the land to their will, to force the land to grow things for their own personal tastes. But gardening for wildlife means loosening the reins of control and growing for reasons beyond aesthetics alone. This requires paying attention to your climate, topography, and soil type, as well as identifying the microclimates and areas of sunlight and shade in your landscape. It also means learning about your existing plant communities and uncovering what species of wildlife share the land where you live. Understanding these characteristics will help you to grow *with* the land and reduce harmful inputs and measures of control.

Climate and Ecoregions

Since 1927, gardeners in the United States have relied on plant hardiness zones to determine which species of plants can thrive in specific regions of the country. These hardiness maps rely on a limited view of plant characteristics determined largely by climate and temperature survivability of plants. This means that areas of Ohio are in the same hardiness zone as areas of California. But many plants that are native to California are not likely to be found growing naturally in Ohio.

While hardiness zones can help us determine whether a plant can survive the climatic conditions of our gardens, they don't tell us whether those plants support wildlife or ecosystem services. That's where ecoregions can

Swallowtail butterfly on bergamot

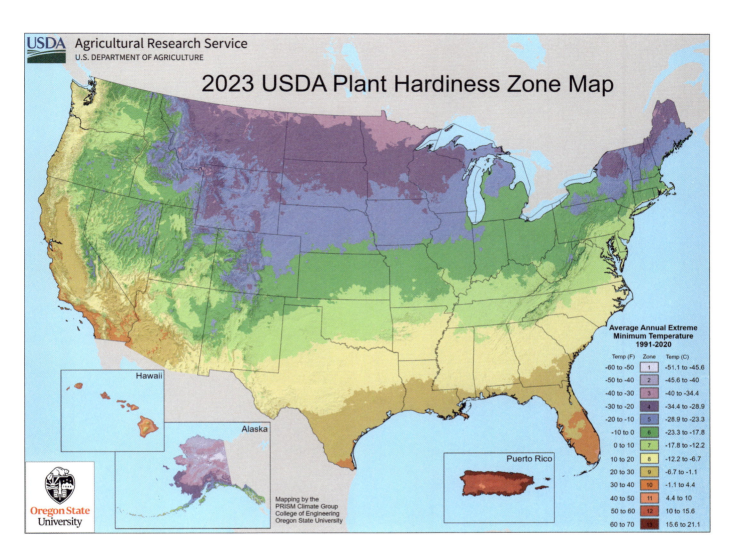

help. An ecoregion is a geographically defined area of land or water that shares similar environmental conditions and distinct ecosystems with a characteristic makeup of plants and wildlife. Species can span multiple ecoregions, but plants and wildlife adapted for one may not thrive within the conditions of another. A quick internet search can help you determine your ecoregion, which will in turn help you uncover which plants are best suited for your garden and which will support biodiversity.

Topography

Topography, which refers to the shape of the land, influences a variety of landscape characteristics, including the health of your soil. Areas with high elevation tend to have well-draining soils (sometimes too well), while low-lying areas may have poorly drained soils that are susceptible to waterlogging. The slope of the land can also influence soil erosion and the types of plants that will thrive in a given area. Slopes are more vulnerable to erosion, which creates thinner soils

← Planting deep-rooted native plants on steep slopes can help to prevent soil erosion while eliminating the need to mow steep areas of your yard.

↓ Low-lying areas are prone to long periods of waterlogging.

over time as the surface of the land is washed away in heavy rains. Planting deep-rooted plants in these areas can help to stabilize soil and prevent erosion. Low-lying areas that are prone to drainage issues, on the other hand, may benefit from water-loving plants that can soak up a lot of moisture, reducing the amount of standing water in your yard after heavy rainfall events.

Soil Type

Just as people have food preferences, different plants have different nutrient and moisture requirements. While some plants prefer sandy, well-draining soils, others are adapted to clay soils that stay wetter for longer during the growing season. Plants uptake nutrients by way of water from the soil, making soil type an important factor in determining what plants will grow well in your wildlife garden and ensuring that you're planting the right species in the right place. Here's a primer on the four main types of soil you might find in your garden.

SANDY SOIL

Sandy soil is characterized by its coarse gritty texture. It has larger particles, resulting in well-draining soil—but depending on what you're hoping to grow, its ability to drain water may come as a disadvantage. Sandy soil can dry out quickly, removing vital nutrients that your plants need to thrive. If you have sandy soil, adding organic matter like compost can improve the soil structure and enhance its ability to retain water and nutrients.

CLAY SOIL

Clay soil has the smallest particles among the four soil types, leading to a dense and heavy texture. It retains moisture well and tends to drain slowly. Clay can become easily compacted and hard when dry, and waterlogged when wet. Though it's highly fertile and rich in nutrients, clay soil can be difficult to work with. Amend with organic matter and avoid working it when wet to improve its structure.

SILT SOIL

Unlike sandy soil, silt soil is characterized by fine-textured, smooth particles. Its particles are smaller than sand but larger than clay, making silt soil feel silky or powdery when dry and slippery when wet. Silt soil is naturally fertile and warms up quickly in the spring, making it suitable for a wide range of plants. But while it offers good moisture retention, it can compact easily. To prevent compaction, avoid tilling and heavy foot traffic when wet.

LOAM SOIL

Loam soil is regarded by many gardeners as the ideal gardening soil because it boasts a balanced mix of sand, silt, and clay. It offers good moisture retention, drainage, and nutrient-holding capacity, and because of its loose and crumbly structure, it provides an excellent environment for plant roots to grow.

OPPOSITE, CLOCKWISE
Sandy soil
....
Clay soil
....
Loam soil
....
Silt soil
....

WHAT'S YOUR TYPE?

Need help determining the makeup of your soil? This activity provides a simple way to determine what type of soil you have in your garden. Different areas of your yard may contain different soil types, so it's a good idea to check a variety of places where you plan to plant.

MATERIALS

A clear, quart-size glass jar with a lid

Soil sample from your garden

Water

A ruler or measuring tape

A soil probe allows you to take a core sample of soil with minimal disturbance to the surrounding area.

PROCEDURE

1. COLLECT A SOIL SAMPLE Choose an area of your landscape where you'd like to test the soil. Using a shovel, dig a hole about 6 to 8 inches deep to collect a representative soil sample. You can also use a soil probe to collect your sample.

2. PREPARE THE SOIL Remove any grass, leaves, rocks, or other debris from the soil sample. Break the soil into small pieces and crumble it or use a sieve or colander to ensure that it's free of clumps or rocks.

3. FILL THE JAR Fill your glass jar about one-third full with your soil sample.

4. ADD WATER Add water to the jar until it's nearly full, leaving just enough space for the lid.

5. SEAL AND SHAKE Secure the lid tightly on the jar, then shake vigorously for a few minutes to ensure that the soil and water are well mixed.

6. SETTLE Place the jar on a level surface and let it sit undisturbed for two to three days. As the soil particles settle, they will separate into layers based on size and weight. These layers will indicate your soil type.

7. OBSERVE THE LAYERS After the settling period, you should see different layers in the jar. The bottom layer will be the heaviest sand particles, followed by a middle layer of silt, and a top layer of clay. Above the layers, you may see a layer of organic matter and some debris.

8. MEASURE THE LAYERS AND CALCULATE SOIL COMPOSITION Use a ruler or measuring tape to measure the thickness of each layer. Calculate the percentage of each soil type in your sample by dividing the thickness of each layer by the total thickness of all layers and multiply by 100. For example:

(Thickness of sand layer/total thickness) × 100 = percentage of sand

(Thickness of silt layer/total thickness) × 100 = percentage of silt

(Thickness of clay layer/total thickness) × 100 = percentage of clay

9. INTERPRET RESULTS If the layers are relatively equal in thickness, you have loam soil. If one layer is dominant, your soil is predominantly composed of that type of soil, for example, mostly clay or mostly sand.

The jar test is an easy and inexpensive way to determine the general composition of your soil at home.

TEST YOUR SOIL

Knowing your soil type is only the beginning of understanding the overall health of your soil. It's also important to understand its nutrient makeup and pH, which will help you in making informed decisions about fertilization and amendments needed for plant health. The essential nutrients that plants take up from the soil through their roots can be broadly categorized into macronutrients and micronutrients. Macronutrients, which include nitrogen, phosphorus, and potassium (denoted as NPK in fertilizer mixes), are consumed in large quantities and play a crucial role in functions like photosynthesis, energy transfer, and root development. Many soils lack macronutrients, requiring soil amendments or fertilization to ensure optimal plant growth. A number of micronutrients, like iron, zinc, and manganese, are also required in smaller amounts for enzyme activities and overall plant health.

Soil pH is a measure of the acidity or alkalinity of soil. A soil's pH level influences the solubility of essential nutrients, which determines a plant's ability to access them. For example, in acidic soils, elements like aluminum and manganese become more available and potentially toxic to plants, while plants in alkaline soils may struggle to access nutrients like iron and phosphorus. Optimal pH levels also create a balanced environment for microbial activity, which is essential for nutrient cycling and the conversion of organic matter into forms that plants can readily absorb. The pH range is 0 (extremely acidic) to 14 (extremely alkaline) with 7.0 being neutral. The pH of most soils ranges from 3.5 to 10.0, and many plants in your home garden will thrive in soils with a pH of 6.0 to 7.0, though some will thrive in more acidic or more alkaline environments. For instance, blueberries, rhododendrons, and conifers prefer acidic soils with a range of 5.0 to 5.5.

To understand the nutrients and pH of your soil, you can perform a soil test. Soil testing kits are available at many garden centers and online retailers, or you can reach out to your county extension office or soil and water conservation district to inquire about soil testing services in your area. Follow the provided instructions for collecting, preparing, and sending your sample. Once you receive the results, you can adjust the soil pH and nutrient levels as needed by amending with compost or other organic materials.

Microclimates

Microclimates are small areas within your yard that have unique environmental conditions, such as temperature, sunlight, and wind exposure. Each microclimate supports its own distinct organisms, and observing how wildlife interact with these areas can be helpful in determining how to attract a variety of species to your garden. Birdbaths, for instance, should be placed in

Having your soil professionally tested will offer expert results that can help you determine the health of your soil.

shadier spots in the yard to keep water cooler and fresher for longer, while nesting boxes should be placed facing northeast so that they avoid strong southerly sunlight and wet winds. To identify the unique microclimates in your yard, start by observing the areas that receive the most sun and shade throughout the day. Pay attention to where wind is the strongest or weakest, as well as areas where water tends to accumulate or drain quickly. A sunny, south-facing ridge, for example, may be warmer and drier than an area beneath a stand of evergreen trees that is noticeably cooler and moister.

Sunlight and Shade

When it comes to plants, some like it hot and sunny, while others thrive in cooler and shadier spots. Plants that require full sun simply cannot thrive in areas of your garden that remain shaded throughout the day. On the other hand, placing a shade-loving plant in a sunny area can lead to plants drying out and overheating as soils lose moisture more quickly. Animals have similar preferences. Insects, spiders, reptiles, and amphibians, for instance, are ectothermic, relying on ambient temperatures to regulate their body temperature. Creating spots where they can bask in the warm sunlight can support these garden residents.

The amount of sunlight your garden receives is primarily influenced by its orientation, or the direction it faces, in relation to the path of the sun as it moves across the sky. This variation in sun exposure is a result of the Earth's rotation and the angle of the sun's rays throughout the day. South-facing gardens receive the most direct sunlight during the day, making them particularly suitable for growing a wide variety

POND PLACEMENT

If you're planning to build a pond as part of your wildlife garden, selecting the right site is critical. Ponds should be constructed in an area that receives at least some sunlight throughout the day. Ponds in heavily shaded areas may not get enough sunlight for aquatic plants to photosynthesize, suffocating the water of oxygen, which aquatic organisms need to thrive. On the other hand, placing small ponds in full sunlight can cause algae to grow out of control. Also consider the pond's depth and size. Larger and deeper ponds will be better at regulating temperature, where smaller, shallower ponds will heat up and cool down more quickly, causing potential problems for water-loving wildlife. Play it safe by choosing an area that receives dappled or indirect sunlight for this water feature.

of sun-loving plants. These are ideal for vegetable gardens and pollinator patches as they provide ample warmth and light so long as they aren't shaded by large trees. East-facing gardens receive gentle morning sun and provide an excellent spot for plants that benefit from milder light and cooler temperatures. Shade-tolerant flowers, like geraniums and columbines, as well as vegetables like lettuces and brassicas, thrive in east-facing gardens. West-facing gardens enjoy the warmth of the afternoon sun, but this sunlight can be intense, making them ideal for sun-loving prairie gardens or pollinator patches. It's essential to monitor these areas, however, as the heat may become excessive during hot summer afternoons, which can stress some plants. North-facing gardens receive the least direct sunlight, especially if tucked tightly against your home or on a slope. This limited exposure makes it challenging to grow sun-hungry plants, but it's perfect for shade-tolerant species like native ferns.

Not sure how much sun your landscape receives? Sketch a rough map of your yard and observe the sunlight exposure at various points of the day, mapping areas of sun and shade. Make your observations during the height of the growing season like midsummer. Choose a few ideal times to observe your yard like 9 a.m., noon, 3 p.m., and 6 p.m. If you're not keen to sketch, take a photo instead. Once you've mapped your yard at various points throughout the day, you'll be able to determine which areas receive full sun, partial sun, and shade. Areas that receive at least six hours of sunlight are perfect for full sun plants. Partial sun plants can be planted in areas of your landscape that receive four to six hours, while shade plants

can be nestled in those that receive four or fewer hours of sunlight.

Plant Communities

If you've not yet taken the time to identify the plants growing in your landscape, now is a great time to start. Plants create the foundation for supporting wildlife. If you have a lot of existing wildflowers and native grasses in your garden, you are likely already attracting a diversity of pollinators. On the other hand, if nut-bearing trees and fruit-bearing shrubs make up the

Understanding how the sun moves across your landscape is essential in determining where plants will thrive and how wildlife may use different areas of your yard. ↗

··········

This north-facing garden receives little sunlight throughout the day but provides an ideal spot for native woodland plants like ferns and trilliums. →

··········

Not feeling great about your plant identification skills? Thanks to modern technology, plant ID is a breeze. Many phone apps can help you get started with identifying the plants in your yard, and some phones even have plant and animal identification capabilities included in the native camera app. Simply snap a photo and let your phone do the rest. If you're still coming up short, try iNaturalist. This science app relies on community-driven identification of plants and animals. With a few decent photos of the leaves, stems, or flowers of a plant, you're almost sure to find someone who can help you pinpoint those tough-to-ID species.

iNaturalist is a great tool for identifying the various plants and animals you observe in your landscape.

START A NATURE JOURNAL

One of the best ways to learn about nature in your own yard is to begin nature journaling. Nature journaling involves keeping a record of the plants, animals, and interactions you observe in your landscape through notes and sketches. By taking time to record these observations, you might begin to notice new patterns and connections that you previously missed. For example, you may learn that bees and other pollinators visit the wild violets that pop up in your lawn each spring. This observation might lead you to forgo mowing during certain times of the year to allow the bees to forage safely. Nature journaling can also help you track the progress of your wildlife garden over time so you can see how things change and evolve as you transform your landscape for nature.

Nature journaling is a great way to uncover how your landscape changes over time while making note of your wildlife visitors.

majority of plant life in your landscape, you might see a lot of birds and small mammals, like chipmunks and squirrels. Identifying the plants in your yard will also help you determine which plants should stay and which should go. You might be surprised to learn that some common ornamental plants, like Japanese barberry and burning bush, are invasive in some regions and can spread to nearby natural areas, outcompeting native vegetation and disrupting the ecosystem. Invasive plants should be removed and replaced with native plants that support wildlife without the threat of disrupting nature.

Wildlife

Throughout the year, spend time walking around your landscape and looking—or listening—for evidence of wildlife. Perhaps you see a lot of birds visiting your feeders during their spring and fall migration. Or maybe you hear owls making midnight calls on spring nights or the screech of red-tailed hawks during summer afternoons. You might notice tracks in freshly fallen snow, which creates the perfect canvas for the pawprints of foxes, raccoons, and coyote. Or the calls of frogs or crickets may sing you to sleep each night. By understanding how wild animals are using your

Fox print in freshly fallen snow

yard, you can select plants and landscape features that are most likely to support them, while avoiding those that may be harmful.

INSTALL A WILDLIFE TRAIL CAMERA

From trail cameras that capture elusive nocturnal creatures like skunks and opossums to bird feeder cameras that closely monitor the birds (and, let's be honest, squirrels), wildlife cameras provide a unique look at who's visiting your garden. You can even install a nesting box with built-in cameras that provide a bird's eye view of activities inside. Recording the behaviors, feeding patterns, and interactions of wildlife will provide valuable insights into the abundance and diversity of species visiting your landscape each day. What's more, you can begin tracking how wildlife visitation shifts over time as you restore ecosystem function to your yard.

When choosing a camera, start by considering what features will be most useful to you. Do you want a camera that can take both photos and video? Is the ability to capture nighttime visitors important? Would you prefer a camera with wi-fi functionality, allowing you to view and download wildlife captures from your phone? Also be sure to consider charging capabilities. Some cameras offer built-in solar panels, harnessing the sun's power to reduce (or eliminate) the need for recharging. Other cameras rely on batteries, which will need to be replaced every so often. Once you decide on the perfect model, position your camera in an area of your landscape where you suspect you'll see a lot of activity, like a water feature or on a tree next to a known wildlife path. Don't be afraid to experiment with placement, moving the camera periodically to uncover new insights about your visitors.

CLOCKWISE
Bird feeder cameras are a great way to get up close and personal with the feathered wildlife you're attracting.

Installing a trail camera in your garden can help uncover the wildlife species visiting your yard at all hours of the day.

A white-tailed deer, skunk, and raccoon all captured on camera.

Chapter 2

LESSEN THE LAWN

Of the infinite possibilities for how neighborhoods could have evolved, the emergence of turfgrass as a monoculture in our home landscapes was a devastating development. Turfgrass provides little ecological benefit, requires carbon- and chemical-intensive inputs, and looks downright dismal when compared to a thriving and colorful alternative of native plant gardens. And yet, in neighborhoods around the world, homeowners and landscape managers tend tediously to these carpets of green turf. Thankfully, the world is finally waking up to the destruction caused by our firm grip on grass.

The Ubiquity of Antiquity

From our home lawns and recreational sports fields to our parks and golf courses, turfgrass covers more than 40 million acres of land in the United States alone, making it the most irrigated crop in the country (Milesi et al., 2005). But how did we come to appreciate these monotonous monocultures? The appeal of short lawns first emerged in 17th century England among wealthy landowners. Lawns became a status symbol because only the wealthy could afford the hired help needed to maintain such monstrosities. Not long after, immigrants brought the idea

From small pollinator patches to woodland understories, native gardens can take a variety of forms to fit your gardening goals and personal aesthetic.
. . . .

of turfgrass lawns to North America, where industrialization—and corporate advertising—bolstered the practice. The advent of tools like lawnmowers meant that lawns were no longer reserved for the posh. Cutting one's own grass became the new norm, and subdivision designers and lawn care companies further reinforced the idea through strategic marketing.

The Cost of Maintaining a Mass of Grass

Each year, Americans spend somewhere around $30 billion on lawn care in an unjustified effort to compete with their next-door neighbor. Coaxed by an endless train of door-to-door salesmen each summer, homeowners are further encouraged to proactively blanket their yards with pesticides in a futile attempt to rid their landscape of creatures in search of the tiniest oasis of habitat where they may rest, refuel, or reproduce. But in many neighborhoods, no such oasis exists. Where once stood forests, now stand homes. Where once flowed streams, now flow pesticides and fertilizers. Patch by patch, natural areas around the world have been overtaken by cities, towns, and neighborhoods. Within these communities, people have uprooted native plants and replaced them with a carpet of green grass. And in doing so, we've destroyed wildlife habitat and disrupted ecological functioning.

To keep grass weed- and pest-free, homeowners apply more pesticides per acre to their yards than farmers apply to crops. Only, farms provide food for a growing global population, where our home landscapes provide scarcely more than competition with the neighbors. It's hard not to fall victim to this Keeping Up with the Joneses mentality. In a sea of perfectly manicured and maintained yards, being the only neighbor gardening for wildlife might seem altogether unneighborly. Whispers about curb appeal and home value might ripple throughout the community when fallen leaves are left to overwinter as a safe haven for wildlife looking for warmth or last season's dried flower stems

TOP, FIRST COLUMN
Lawns are the most irrigated crop in the United States.

LEFT
Moving away from a turfgrass landscape could be as easy as following the natural tendencies of your yard, like leaving the leaves—or the needles.

Plant communities act as carbon sinks, or areas that absorb more carbon from the atmosphere than they release. Globally, forests soak up nearly 8 billion metric tons of CO_2 per year, more than twice as much as they emit (Harris et al., 2021). Similarly, wetlands and native grasslands like prairies can sequester, or store, up to several tons of carbon per acre, depending on the type and quality of the habitat. By contrast, turfgrass lawns are major contributors to greenhouse gas emissions because their benefits as carbon sinks are usually outweighed by the carbon-intensive management required to keep them up to snuff. One study found that gasoline-powered lawn and garden equipment was responsible for 26.7 million tons of pollutants in 2011, which accounted for 24 to 45 percent of all non-road gasoline emissions that year. Gasoline-powered landscape maintenance equipment like leaf blowers, trimmers, and edgers accounted for 43 percent of volatile organic compounds and half of fine particulate matter. Among the worst offenders are lawn care tools that use two-stroke engines (Banks & McConnell, 2015).

· ·

As forests are replaced with developments, the world loses important carbon sinks.

are left standing for opportunistic bees in search of the perfect nest.

Weeding, feeding, mowing, blowing, cutting, trimming, watering. The American Time Use Survey notes that the average American spends 70 hours on lawn care each year, collectively pouring around 8 billion gallons of water on their lawns each day. We've even grown fond of maintaining these grass landscapes in drought-stricken and dry areas of the world where they are not only unnatural, but impractical and selfish too. Adding insult to injury, much of the equipment we use to maintain grass creates a racket, breaking through the silence of every perfect summer morning with the whirring of the mower and shattering the tranquility of every fall weekend with the blasting of the blower. To put it simply, our home landscapes have created ecological deserts not fit for wildlife and barely fit for people. We have rendered ourselves distinctly separate from the nature that surrounds us. But we can change that.

Lawn care, like leaf blowing, can contribute to both carbon emissions and noise pollution.

· ·

Let Go of Grass

At the heart of homegrown conservation is letting go of turfgrass. Lessening—or altogether ridding—your yard of turf opens a world of possibilities that challenge conventional landscape design and support nature and wildlife while helping to fight the impacts of climate change. To accomplish this, you might be tempted to store away the mower and let nature rebound on its own. But transitioning your yard away from turfgrass is going to take a bit more strategy. Scaling back routine mowing won't magically bring nature back. Instead, you'll likely find yourself in a sea of non-native and invasive plants whose seeds have been lurking beneath the surface of the soil waiting for their chance to shine. Or worse, you may end up with a hefty fine from your township as punishment for your newly unkempt yard. Rest assured, a beautiful and functional non-turfgrass-landscape is within grasp, but you need to establish a plan to get there.

Start Small

Transitioning lawn away from grass can be time-intensive and costly. If you're in a position to rip up your entire lawn and plant native flowering plants, that's great! But this route isn't always feasible or realistic. And that's perfectly okay—start small. Pick a patch of your yard and plan how you might transition it away from grass. If it's a shaded area, consider planting a small woodland garden. If your yard is bright and sunny, planting a small pollinator plot might make more sense. Starting small will help you reach your goals without the project seeming too overwhelming. As resources allow, you can

continue to grow your efforts, learning from mistakes and experimenting as you go. After all, learning is part of the fun.

Make Your Bed

Once you pick an area of your yard to replace your lawn with native plants, it's time to make your bed—your garden bed. There are a few ways to remove turfgrass for garden bed prep, and each method comes with its own set of pros and cons. The route you choose will depend on a variety of factors including the size of the area you're preparing, how much time and energy you'd like to invest in the process, how quickly you'd like to replant the area, your

FROM TOP
Storing away the lawn mower won't bring you the native garden of your dreams.

Planting a pollinator patch is a great way to support wildlife if you have a small, sunny yard.

tolerance for using herbicides, your budget, and your physical ability. Here are a few methods to consider for taking out your turf.

SOD REMOVAL

Sod removal is best for those planning to stay away from chemicals or those in a hurry to lessen the lawn. While it's the quickest way to remove turf, sod removal is also the most labor-intensive, especially if you're planning to do it manually. You can rent a sod cutter, but keep in mind these machines are often gas-powered and contribute to greenhouse gas emissions through burning fuel. If you're looking for a greener option, manual cutting is a great choice. To remove sod, it's best to water your landscape a few days prior to removal to make the ground easier to work. You can rent a kick-type manual sod cutter, which will help pull up strips of sod, or use a flathead shovel to accomplish the same end result.

LASAGNA GARDENING

Lasagna gardening is a method of creating no-till, no-dig garden beds by stacking compostable materials like cardboard, leaves, kitchen scraps, and newspaper to suffocate the grass. To create a lasagna garden, you'll want to layer brown materials (those with a high carbon to nitrogen ratio) with green materials (those with a low carbon to nitrogen ratio). Together, these materials will break down, creating rich soil that's perfect for planting. Start by mowing your lawn as short as possible. Next, lay down a layer of cardboard (a thick layer of newspaper works well too). You'll want to be sure to use boxes that are 100% recyclable and free from inks and waxy coatings that could contaminate

FROM TOP
Cardboard is effective at smothering grass and will break down over time, adding carbon back into the soil.

Lasagna gardening allows you to repurpose materials in your landscape, like fallen leaves.

If you're itching to plant before the layer of cardboard has effectively killed grass, cover with several inches of compost and start planting.

your soil with harmful chemicals. Also be sure to remove tape, shipping labels, and staples from any boxes you intend to use in the garden.

To ensure your grass is properly suffocated, layer the edges of your cardboard to prevent gaps grass can sneak into. Before adding your next layer, water the cardboard with a good soaking to help this layer stay in place. Next, add a two-to-three-inch layer of green material like kitchen scraps, grass clippings, or manure. After this green layer comes another layer of brown material. This layer should be composed of materials like fallen leaves, pine needles, or straw. Continue alternating layers at least twice more so you have a total of four layers, excluding the initial layer of cardboard. While you don't need to be exact in your ratios, you should aim for a brown to green ratio of about 2:1, or two parts brown to one part green material. The downside to lasagna gardening is the time it takes for materials to break down and create soil that's ready for new plants. From start to finish, it could take six to twelve months before your new bed is ready. If you're itching to plant right away, add a hefty layer of compost and start planting.

SOLARIZATION

Solarization is one of the easier methods of killing off grass and preparing garden beds to welcome native plants. However, it can take a bit of time. Solarization is a process that uses heat from the sun to kill vegetation by covering it with clear plastic during the hot summer months. To solarize your lawn, mow grass as short as possible and water the area until the soil is moist to a depth of 12 to 18 inches. Watering not only promotes the germination of seeds which will

NO NEED TO TILL

· ·

Tilling is an oft-recommended practice when preparing a new garden bed. But is it necessary? In a word, no. Tilling not only disturbs the soil by dredging up weed seeds and releasing stored carbon, which contributes to climate change, but it can also increase soil erosion. It's best to use no-till or no-dig methods of garden bed prep like mulching to maintain soil health.

· ·

later be killed in the solarization process, but it also helps to increase soil temperatures since moisture helps conduct heat. Once watered, lay a clear plastic sheet over the area of grass you'd like to kill and ensure all edges are firmly secured. Clear plastic is more effective than black plastic at trapping heat due to the greenhouse effect. Opaque plastics will not let enough light through to heat the soil temperature enough to kill vegetation. Depending on daily temperatures, you can expect grass to die off in six to eight weeks. Once solarized, remove and recycle, or dispose of, all plastic waste from your yard. You can plant seeds or transplants directly into the soil, or add a layer of compost before planting.

MULCHING

While solarization and lasagna gardening have been touted as easy and chemical-free ways to kill the lawn, they come with downsides. These methods ultimately suffocate and kill turfgrass, but they can also block the ability of water to filter into the soil and reduce the gas exchange needed for the diversity of life that dwells within the soil ecosystem. In other words, while these

ALTERNATIVES TO GRASS

Ready to say goodbye to grass but still want to maintain the traditional appearance of a lawn? There are a variety of alternatives for homeowners who wish to maintain a healthy, green landscape while breaking away from the monotony of grass. Clover forms a lush, low-maintenance groundcover while providing a food source for pollinators like bees, and clover's nitrogen-fixing roots help to enrich the soil. Creeping thyme, a drought-tolerant and sun-loving perennial, requires minimal maintenance, boasts a spicy fragrance, and like many plants in the mint family, attracts a diversity of bees and other polli-nators. If you want to think outside the traditional box, give moss a try. Moss creates a carpet-like appearance and thrives in shady areas like under the canopy of trees. Its ability to retain moisture also helps to maintain a cool, damp environment, which benefits amphibians and insects. While not all of these options may be native to your region, they provide a myriad of benefits to wildlife while reducing carbon and chemical-intensive inputs, making them a superior choice compared to turfgrass.

Clover can be a great alternative to turfgrass in the home landscape, but like turfgrass, mono-cultures of any species should be avoided.

methods are effective for killing grass, they are also effective at killing other things in the soil too, including beneficial microbes and soil-dwelling organisms.

Research from The Garden Professors, a group of university professors dedicated to translating scientific information for gardeners, shows that the most effective way to kill grass naturally without damaging soil health is to scalp the lawn by mowing as closely to the ground as possible, then mulch the area with a deep layer of freshly cut arborist wood chips. Wood chips can be sourced from local arborists, and you might be lucky enough to find them for free by calling around to local landscaping companies. To effectively block sunlight from reaching eager weeds, woodchips should be layered to a depth of 8 to 18 inches, though many gardeners note that some plants, like Bermuda grass, will still find their way through. Check on progress every few weeks and when the grass is sufficiently killed and the ground is easy enough to dig, it's time to prepare for planting. You'll need to remove the bulk of the remaining wood chips to ensure that your seeds or plants are planted directly into soil. During this time, keep an eye on persistent weeds that might use this as an opportunity to break dormancy from being blanketed by the woodchips. Remove weeds promptly to avoid them from recolonizing the garden bed. After planting, you can mulch the beds with a small layer of the wood chips you previously removed to help retain moisture in the new garden bed.

Despite the upsides to mulching, it can come with a hefty price tag, especially if you're unable to source chips for free. An added consideration is the manual labor involved in spreading a deep layer of wood chips. If you're working on a large garden bed, you could be looking at spreading tens of yards of mulch. For those with limited mobility, or a limited budget to pay a crew, this method could be prohibitive, especially considering that the wood chips will need to be moved several times over the course of suffocating turfgrass—once for the initial application, again for planting, and one final time if you choose to add a layer of mulch back to your newly planted garden bed.

HERBICIDES

Killing the lawn with herbicides is one of the easier and quicker methods of turfgrass removal, especially if you're planning to kill a large area of grass. However, chemical applications are not the most environmentally friendly choice as they involve spraying chemicals on your lawn, which can impact wildlife and non-target plants. Glyphosate, which is marketed as Roundup, is one of the most widely used herbicides and is a top choice among farmers and gardeners alike as it is a non-selective herbicide, meaning it will kill most plants with which it comes into contact. Though it is considered non-toxic to humans when used in accordance with its label, studies show that prolonged exposure to the herbicide can negatively impact aquatic organisms. Unless necessary, more environmentally friendly methods of turfgrass removal are recommended.

Roundup is a popular choice among homeowners for killing grass, but chemicals in the wildlife garden should be used judiciously and only when other options have been exhausted.

Chapter 3

GROW NATIVE

Plants are everywhere around us. But, if you're like most people, there's a chance you might not be able to name many of the plant species you see every day. Unless you're an avid gardener or a naturalist, you might suffer from a condition known as plant blindness, a phenomenon that describes the human tendency to ignore plant species. Differentiating between oak and maple leaves may come easy. But when the trees have been stripped bare by winter's frost, you might struggle to notice the seemingly subtle differences in crown shape and bark texture of these magnificent trees. These differences, however, are not so subtle for wildlife.

Plants with a Purpose

Animals depend on plants, from seeds and nuts to berries and leaves for survival. Plants create the foundation of nearly every ecosystem on Earth, harvesting the sun's energy to create sugars, which provide food for other organisms, and furnishing shelter for wildlife to raise their young. Birds nest in trees. Rabbits and deer find protection among the tall grasses in prairies and meadows. And insects find nutrition among the blooms that decorate

Without plants to provide food and shelter, wildlife cannot thrive in our home gardens.

our landscapes. Unfortunately, there's often a mismatch between the plants we're growing in our communities and the plants that animals need to thrive.

While many animals are generalists, tolerating a wide range of foods and habitats, others are specialists, thriving only within narrow environmental conditions and feeding only on a small selection of foods with which they evolved over thousands of years. People are generalists. We can tolerate a wide range of conditions, from dry deserts to humid rain-forests. We can also thrive on a wide range of diets from plant-based to almost exclusively fast food (though the latter isn't recommended). But animals are not so lucky. When we replace the plants that wildlife specialists rely on for food and habitat with non-native plants, we destine them to an uncertain future.

The Downside to Non-native Plants

European colonists began introducing new plants to the American landscape as soon as they arrived. Many of these plants were brought here intentionally for use as food, medicine, or for ornamental purposes. Some plants, however, were introduced accidentally in ballast water from ships, in animal feed, or in grain. Since the early days of colonization, plant introductions haven't slowed. The Office of Seed and Plant Introduction, the first official branch of the United States Department of Agriculture, has introduced more than 200,000 types of non-native plants into the United States since

(continued on page 46)

DECODING PLANT LINGO

There's no shortage of words we use to describe plants and their characteristics. Here are a few plant words worth knowing.

NATIVE PLANT A plant that is a part of the balance of nature that has developed over hundreds or thousands of years in a particular region or ecosystem. Only plants found in the United States before European colonization are considered native to this country.

NATIVAR A cultivar of a native plant cultivated for specific traits like bloom color, size, or pest and disease resistance.

WILD-TYPE or STRAIGHT SPECIES A native plant that is regionally specific and found naturally occurring in the wild without cultivation or hybridization.

NON-NATIVE PLANT A plant introduced with human help (intentionally or accidentally) to a new place or new type of habitat where it was not previously found.

NATURALIZED PLANT A non-native plant that does not need human help to reproduce and maintain itself over time in an area where it is not native.

EXOTIC PLANT A plant not native to the continent on which it is now found.

OPPORTUNISTIC NATIVE PLANT A native plant that can take advantage of disturbance to the soil or existing vegetation to spread quickly and out-compete the other plants on the disturbed site.

WEED A plant (native or non-native) that is not valued in the place where it is growing.

INVASIVE PLANT A plant that is both non-native and able to establish on many sites, grow quickly, and spread to the point of disrupting plant communities or ecosystems.

NOXIOUS WEED A plant that can directly or indirectly injure or cause damage to crops, livestock, or other interests of agriculture, irrigation, navigation, natural resources, public health, or the environment.

MILKWEED SUPPORTS MORE THAN MONARCHS

The monarch butterfly has long been hailed as a poster child of insect conservation. For more than 40 years, populations of the large black and orange butterflies have been declining. Populations of western monarchs, which overwinter in California, have declined 99 percent from the 1980s, while eastern monarchs, which migrate to central Mexico, have plummeted around 80 percent during that time.

Monarch butterflies are specialist pollinators that lay their eggs on a sole family of plants—the milkweed family. Without milkweed, monarchs cannot reproduce. Unfortunately, milkweed has been replaced by non-native ornamental plants in many home landscapes, and intensifying agricultural production has replaced large swaths of monarch habitat throughout the nation. Urban development, pesticide use, disease, and climate change have added to the growing list of threats that put monarchs and other wildlife at risk.

Fortunately, rallying cries from invertebrate conservation organizations, like the Xerces Society, have effectively united the nation in supporting their comeback by planting milkweed and reducing pesticide use across the United States. But attempts to save a single species can sometimes create unintended—and even harmful—consequences for other wildlife. Milkweed, for example, supports more than monarchs. Insects like red milkweed beetles and milkweed bugs, which are both native

to North America, also rely on the plant, but many gardeners consider these insects pests. A web search for "milkweed pests" will populate a long list of articles detailing how to protect milkweed from these less desirable species.

Milkweed is not meant for monarchs alone. In fact, one study found that monarch butterfly egg and early instar survivability was higher on host plants where a greater number and variety of other non-predatory arthropods were observed (Stevenson et al., 2021). The study's authors suggest that the presence of a diversity of prey on milkweed allowed possible predators to overlook monarch eggs and larvae in search of other prey, reinforcing the importance of supporting the whole ecosystem over just a single species.

CLOCKWISE

Monarch caterpillars are specialists that rely on the availability of milkweed to reproduce.

Monarch butterflies lay their eggs on plants in the milkweed family.

Closeup of monarch egg on milkweed leaf

Milkweed bugs on milkweed

(continued from page 42)

its establishment in 1898. With today's global economy, it's easier than ever to transport plants from one side of the world to the other. But there is a bit of good news about this influx of non-native plants. According to the United States Environmental Protection Agency, only around 10 percent of the species introduced into new ecosystems survive, and of those that do, only 10 percent (or 1 percent of the original species introduced) become invasive. That's a relief. Or is it?

Beauty Is More Than Bloom Deep

Just because a non-native plant doesn't become invasive doesn't mean wildlife will benefit from its presence in the landscape. The addition of a non-native plant into a new community likely displaced another plant—a native one—that wildlife depended on for food, shelter, or reproduction. As neighborhoods were constructed across the country, forests were cleared, meadows were mowed, and wetlands were filled to make room for towns and cities. Through this development, native plants were replaced with a palette of carefully curated non-native, ornamental species.

Introduced to North America hundreds of years ago, tulips are non-native but not known to be invasive or problematic in the American landscape. ↑

....

While pollinators may visit non-native blooms, many non-native plants don't provide the same benefits as native species. →

....

Replacing communities of native plants with non-native ornamentals severs the evolutionary connection between plants and animals, reducing non-native plants to little more than botanical decorations in our landscapes, as many of these species provide few, if any, ecological benefits.

Gardening with Native Plants

Gardening with native plants is one of the best ways to support wildlife at home. It can also reduce the need for artificial pesticides and

fertilizers and curb climate-intensive landscape management practices like routine mowing and watering. But choosing native plants might not be as simple as heading to your nearest nursery and selecting any plant that says "native." Here are some considerations for making the most of native plants at home.

Plant for Your Ecoregion

Just as people have transported non-native plants around the world, so too have we moved native plants within countries and states. But a plant's ability to grow in one part of the country doesn't determine its suitability to grow in another. Imagine living in a warm region of the world your entire life. One day, you're forced to move across the country to a cold region that receives more snowfall in an hour than you've seen in your entire life. Although you're still in the same country, you're in an entirely different ecoregion, and you might struggle to adapt to your new environmental conditions.

What's native to the western United States might not be native to the eastern part of the country. Even plants native to one region of a state might not be native to another area of the same state. For this reason, it's best to select plant species that are native to your ecoregion. Planting species that originated in your ecoregion means they'll be more resilient to local weather and soil conditions, often reducing the need for watering, fertilizers, and pesticides. When shopping for native plants, it's sometimes difficult to determine a plant's origin, especially since many big-box garden centers label plants "native" if it grows anywhere within the borders of the country where it's being sold. Before you head to the nearest

Native plant gardens are often criticized for being messy, but with proper placement and design, they can jibe with your personal aesthetic.

WHERE TO FIND NATIVE PLANTS

· ·

Over the years, native gardening has grown in popularity. Nowadays, many garden centers, both big and small, offer native plants for sale. You may also have luck finding native plants available through plant sales hosted by local nature centers, arboreta, and soil and water conservation districts. Ordering plants by mail is another option, though shipping may drive up costs and create unnecessary carbon emissions. If you're feeling overwhelmed by choosing native plants for your garden, many states have native plant societies that offer loads of educational resources and local plant lists. Pollinator Partnership, a non-profit whose mission is to promote the health of pollinators, also offers lists of native plants by ecoregion. These can be great places to start when identifying which plants to select for your landscape.

· ·

nursery, identify your ecoregion, and make a list of plants that are native to your area.

Grow a Diversity of Plants

When designing your native plant garden, you're bound to fall in love with a few select plants. Perhaps it's the reliable blooms of purple coneflower, or maybe you're more into the sunny blossoms of goldenrod or black-eyed Susans. Whatever your preference, it's important to avoid a monoculture of your favorite plant. Instead, design a native plant garden that offers ecological interest and importance throughout the year. A greater diversity of plant species will equate to a greater diversity of wildlife that you're helping to support.

Animals need food year-round. It's not enough to offer them a summer buffet of blooms but leave their dinner plates empty for the rest of the year. Planting a variety of species will offer wildlife a feast of options all year long. When planning your garden, include a diversity of early spring blooms that will help sustain the season's first pollinators as they awake from their winter slumber. Also plant a palette of summer-blooming flowers, shrubs, and trees that will give way to seeds, fruits, and nuts that will support wildlife throughout the cooler fall and winter months.

Just like people, many animals' diets evolve as they grow older. Human babies start life on an exclusively liquid diet of milk or formula, but toddlers begin to enjoy a range of solid foods that grows ever more diverse as they age. Animals are similar. Planting a variety of nectaring plants for pollinators is great, but if they don't have host plants where they can lay their eggs, they won't be able to complete their

← Spring-blooming plants, like this eastern redbud, provide a food source for early emerging pollinators.

↓ As late-blooming wild-flowers, goldenrods offer pollinators an important food source well into the fall months.

CAN A NATIVE PLANT BE INVASIVE?

By definition, a native plant cannot be invasive. However, climate change is creating conditions in which some native plants, like poison ivy, can grow a bit more aggressively in some areas. Definitions aside, if a plant becomes problematic where it's growing, it might be time to think about a management plan.

full life cycle. Black swallowtail butterflies, for instance, enjoy sipping nectar from a variety of flowers, including milkweed, phlox, and zinnias, but caterpillars of this species thrive on plants in the carrot family, like parsley, dill, and fennel. Your wildlife garden should include a selection of native plants that will support a variety of species throughout their entire life cycle.

Also be sure to plant for a diversity of wildlife. Planting for pollinators has been all the rage for many years, and supporting our pollinators is of the utmost importance if we'd like to continue filling our dinner plates with a variety of delicious produce. But planting for non-pollinating wildlife is important too, which means thinking about the various forms and structures that plants provide as shelter in the garden. When choosing which plants make the cut for your yard, include an assortment of types and sizes. For instance, tall grasses provide safe spaces for small mammals as they forage for food, while the dense foliage of coniferous trees and shrubs creates cover for birds and other wildlife seeking protection from hungry predators.

FROM TOP

Sky blue asters are host plants for the pearl crescent butterfly and the wavy-lined emerald moth.

Pearl crescent butterfly

Wavy-lined emerald moth

Cutting Costs

Replacing your lawn with native plants can be expensive. There's no need to replace your entire lawn overnight. Start small and expand your native garden as time and resources allow. While buying larger plants, like those in one-to-two-gallon pots, will provide instant gratification, they can quickly drain the bank. Instead, consider buying plugs or small-sized seedlings. Some online retailers sell pre-packaged native plant kits with plugs that are selected for site characteristics like light conditions and soil type. These native plant kits are carefully curated to attract wildlife like native birds and pollinators. A seed mix is another cost-effective option for starting your native plant garden. The downside

of growing a garden from seed is the lack of control over which plant grows where, but if you're okay giving up control, starting a native garden from a seed mix can be a wonderful and inexpensive option for supporting wildlife.

FROM TOP
Trees and dense shrubs provide cover for birds like this juvenile blue jay.

Buying smaller plants can help reduce upfront costs of installing a new garden.

PLANT AN OAK TREE

· ·

According to the Chinese proverb, the best time to plant a tree was 20 years ago. The second-best time is now. But just what kind of tree should you plant? If you're interested in supporting wildlife, the answer is easy: an oak. From the shelter they provide to nesting birds to the nuts they provide to hungry mammals, the benefits of oaks are vast. In fact, oak species collectively support more species of butterflies and moths than any other genus of tree (Tallamy & Shropshire, 2009), and by supporting butterflies and moths, you'll also be supporting a diversity of birds and other wildlife that depend on caterpillars as an important food source. As a bonus, oaks are also great at sequestering carbon, so you can support wildlife while helping to mitigate climate change—a true win-win!

· ·

Nativars: Good or Bad?

Native cultivars, sometimes called nativars, are native plants that have been selectively bred for particular human-desired traits like bloom color, size, or pest resistance. In many big-box garden centers, nativars with flashy names outcompete wild-type, or straight, native species for sales. But do they outcompete wild-type species in the benefits they provide to wildlife? Studies suggest that it depends. Native cultivars that have been bred for atypical bloom shape, like double-flowering coneflowers, fare poorly in their ability to attract pollinators when compared to wild-type species. Similarly, native plant species that have been bred to produce purple instead of green leaves are shown to be less palatable to caterpillars. But in other studies, native cultivars have proven to be more appealing than straight species for some insects.

Wild-type plants are those grown from seeds of plants that grew in the wild. Because they were open pollinated, wild types exhibit genetic diversity that native cultivars lack. Native cultivars are often propagated from cuttings, which result in a clone of the parent plant. Cloning plants ensures that retailers are able to provide the same plant again and again, with no variance, but these clones offer no genetic diversity and provide plants with little defense in adapting to local conditions over time. Ultimately, when making decisions about what to include in your native plant garden, go for wild-type species that are specific to your ecoregion when possible. But don't fret about including a few flashy nativars in your landscape, especially when those newcomers are nestled amongst native species that local wildlife know and love.

Sleep, Creep, Leap

In native gardening, patience really is a virtue as it can take a few years for native perennials to take off. When frustration that your garden isn't quite as lush as you might have imagined starts to set in, remember the sleep, creep, leap rule. Perennials generally spend their first year establishing a solid root system, which means you might be disappointed in the lack of foliage and beautiful blooms. By year two, the plant will still spend energy growing a deep root system, but you can expect to start seeing blooms and more foliage. In year three, the plant should begin to reach its full potential. Just remember, your relationship with your native garden will be more of a slow burn rather than a love-at-first-sight type of romance.

A newly installed native plant garden can look a little lackluster, but in a few years, it will be a thriving oasis for wildlife.

Chapter 4

ELIMINATE INVASIVES

Invasive plant takeovers might sound like a sci-fi concept, but they can be a real-life ecological nightmare. These pesky plants can wreak havoc on natural areas, causing devasting impacts to wildlife and biodiversity. With the right knowledge and tools, you can prevent the spread of invasive species and help native plant communities thrive in your own yard and beyond. But first things first, let's clear up a common misconception. Not all non-native plants are bad. In fact, many non-native plants coexist peacefully with native species and bring beauty to the garden. But when non-native plants become invasive, that's when things go awry.

What Are Invasive Plants?

Invasive plants are non-native species that are introduced to a new environment and have the ability to rapidly reproduce and spread. These plants have a knack for outcompeting native plant species for resources like sunlight, water, and nutrients, and they also exhibit aggressive growth habits and fast growth rates, and often have efficient reproductive strategies. With few natural predators to keep them in check and the ability to tolerate a wide range of environmental conditions, they can rapidly colonize new areas and quickly dominate local ecosystems. Once

Phragmites australis, also known as common reed, is an invasive plant in the United States that invades wetland habitats.

CLOCKWISE
Invasive plants, like the multiflora rose pictured to the left of this red-winged blackbird, outcompete native vegetation, which can impact the ability of wildlife to find food and shelter.

Burning bush and Japanese honeysuckle, both popular invasive shrubs in the eastern United States, are readily spread by birds that enjoy feasting on their fruits.

Japanese honeysuckle berries

established, some invasive plant species can even alter soil chemistry, nutrient cycling, and hydrological cycles, further reducing the diversity and abundance of native plants, which in turn can impact the insects, birds, and mammals that depend on those plants for food and habitat.

Evasive Invasives

Invasive plants are often introduced to new areas by human activity. They may be intentionally planted for ornamental or agricultural purposes or accidentally introduced through contaminated soil, water, or seed shipments. Once established, these weedy invaders can spread in a variety of ways. Many invasive plants produce copious amounts of seeds that can be carried by wind, water, animals, or people. Other plants reproduce asexually by forming new plants from stem fragments, rhizomes, or other plant parts. No matter how plants spread, one thing remains true: invasive plants have a knack for jumping borders and escaping from cultivated landscapes, establishing themselves in nearby natural areas. Even if you don't see the impact of invasive plants locally, birds and other wildlife can transport seeds miles away where your prized garden plants may devastate local ecology.

Impacts of Invasive Plants

The impacts of invasive plants are far-reaching and can have serious consequences for the environment and the economy. Ecologically, invasive plants outcompete native species, reduce biodiversity, and disrupt ecosystem function. Invasive plants can also limit recreational opportunities

and diminish the aesthetic value of natural areas. Plants like kudzu and Japanese knotweed, for example, can grow so quickly and aggressively that they take over entire landscapes, making it difficult for people to enjoy outdoor activities like hiking, fishing, and camping. Additionally, invasive plants can damage infrastructure, such as roads and buildings, which can lead to safety concerns and costly repairs. Economically, invasive plants reduce crop yields and increase the cost of production for farmers, ultimately impacting the entire food supply chain. All told, invasive species cost the global economy around $423 billion per year and have played an important role in 60 percent of plant and animal extinctions, according to a 2023 report from the Intergovernmental Science-Policy Platform on Biodiversity and Ecosystem Services.

FORESTS UNDER THREAT

Prior to European colonization, nearly one half of what is now the United States was forested. Since then, around 75 percent of virgin forests have been destroyed. Reforestation efforts have helped put trees back on the landscape, and habitat conservation has helped protect our remaining old growth forests. But our woodlands are still under threat. Today, forests are filled with invasive plants. Garlic mustard, a biennial flower that creates carpets of monocultures in lowland forests, outcompetes ephemeral wildflowers, threatening the pollinators that depend on those early spring blooms for food. Invasive shrubs, like multiflora rose and non-native honeysuckles, block sunlight from reaching the forest floor, stifling the regeneration of native trees. In glaciated areas of the East, invasive earthworms overconsume the duff layer, leaving the forest floor barren for wildlife that rely on this leafy layer of habitat for food and shelter. As invasive species overtake our forests, the entire structure and composition of these ecosystems are changing, and their ability to support native wildlife is diminishing, making it ever more important to stop the spread of invasives.

FROM TOP

Garlic mustard invades lowland forests, where it outcompetes spring wildflowers like Virginia bluebells.

Virginia bluebells paint the forest floor with shades of blue and pink each spring in a healthy woodland.

THE BRADFORD PEAR: A CAUTIONARY TALE

The Bradford pear has a history rooted in good intentions, but its story serves as a cautionary tale of using non-native ornamental plants to decorate our landscapes. Introduced to the United States in the early 1960s, the Bradford pear quickly gained popularity as an urban and suburban ornamental tree due to its symmetrical shape, early spring blooms, and vibrant fall foliage, which made it a favored choice for landscaping projects. Though the tree was bred to be a sterile cultivar, people soon learned that it could cross-pollinate with other pear cultivars that were later introduced to compensate for the Bradford pear's weak branching structure, leading to the production of fertile hybrids.

Over time, these hybrids began to escape cultivation and spread aggressively into natural areas, roadsides, and disturbed landscapes. Recognizing the ecological impact of the invasive tree, many conservationists have advised against planting them and encouraged the use of native alternatives instead, like redbud, red buckeye, or native dogwoods. In some states, Bradford pear is now illegal to propagate and sell.

Know What You Grow

Overcoming the impact of invasive plants may seem overwhelming, but removing and replacing these harmful species from your landscape can help stop the spread and reduce the likelihood of future invasions. After all, many common invasive plants started as ornamental garden plants that refused to play nicely with others. To learn more about which species of plants are invasive in your area, check with local conservation organizations or your state's department of natural resources. These organizations often maintain lists of invasive species that are known to be problematic in your region, along with information about how to control or remove them.

Monitor and Remove Plant Bullies

Be on the lookout for signs of invasive plants in your garden. If you spot a problem plant, take action right away. Don't wait for it to spread and cause damage. Attending to aggressive plants early will reduce the likelihood of a much larger problem in the future, so take time to properly identify the problem plant and research the best methods of control for that species. While some plants can simply be pulled from the ground, others might need a bit of extra work to remove. After all, invasive plants become invasive for a reason—their tough-as-nails characteristics are what led to them becoming a problem in the first place. And that means you might need to put up a bit of a fight to get them under control.

MANUAL CONTROL

Manual removal involves physically pulling or digging out an invasive plant by hand. This

the essence. Plants should always be pulled or otherwise removed before they go to seed, so you don't unintentionally plant a whole new generation of invasive plants as seeds are shaken loose.

MECHANICAL CONTROL

Mechanical removal involves using tools such as chainsaws, loppers, or mowers to remove an invasive plant. While chainsaws and loppers can be effective for controlling woody species like Asian bittersweet or honeysuckle, mowing can be effective for invasive grasses like Japanese stiltgrass. Mechanical control of invasive plants can sometimes be expensive and may require specialized equipment and training. Using heavy equipment like mowers can also disturb the soil and damage surrounding vegetation, so

method can be effective for small infestations of herbaceous invasive species like garlic mustard, but it can be labor-intensive and may not be practical for larger infestations or for woody plants. It's important to remove as much of the root system as possible to prevent the plant from resprouting. Depending on where you live, springtime can be an ideal time for invasive plant pulling as the ground tends to be soft from snowmelt. But remember that time is of

CLOCKWISE

If you identify an invasive plant in your yard, like this Japanese honeysuckle, make a plan to remove and replace it with a native species that will better support wildlife, like black chokeberry, witch hazel, or spice bush.

Hailing from Eurasia, dame's rocket is an invasive plant in many US states that is often included in wildflower seed mixes, underscoring the importance of knowing what you grow.

Garlic mustard should be pulled during the spring before they've gone to seed to avoid spreading seeds.

COMMON ORNAMENTAL PLANTS
THAT TURNED INVASIVE

JAPANESE BARBERRY (*Berberis thunbergii*)
Originally introduced as an ornamental shrub due to its attractive red foliage and adaptability to various soil conditions, Japanese barberry has since spread aggressively to natural areas. This invasiveness is largely attributed to the shrub's prolific seed production and the fact that its berries are consumed and spread readily by birds, facilitating its rapid colonization of natural ecosystems. Japanese barberry forms dense thickets that alter soil composition, hinder the growth of native plants, and disrupt local ecosystems. Additionally, it poses a threat to human health by providing ideal habitat for ticks that carry Lyme disease.

PURPLE LOOSESTRIFE (*Lythrum salicaria*)
Native to Eurasia, purple loosestrife was popularized in the United States as an ornamental plant thanks to its striking purple flowers. But the plant's ability to produce a large number of seeds, as well as its capacity to spread via its root system, has allowed it to rapidly colonize wetlands, where it has displaced native vegetation. Purple loosestrife forms dense stands that clog waterways and reduce the diversity of native wetland plants, which in turn impacts the many species of wildlife that rely on these highly biodiverse habitats.

NORWAY MAPLE (*Acer platanoides*) Originally brought to the United States for its attractive foliage and shade-providing characteristics, Norway maple has spread aggressively and displaced native plant species. This invasive tree monopolizes resources like water, sunlight, and nutrients, often outcompeting native maple species that provide essential wildlife habitat and ecosystem stability. Additionally, the dense canopy created by Norway maples shades out understory plants, reducing native tree regeneration and suppressing the growth of native wildflowers, both of which alter species composition in the understory of forests.

BURNING BUSH (*Euonymus alatus*) Also known as winged euonymus, burning bush was introduced to the United States from Asia in the 19th century as an ornamental shrub appreciated for its vibrant fall foliage. It has since become a problematic invasive species due to its rapid growth, prolific seed production, and adaptability to various habitats, which have allowed it to escape cultivation and spread aggressively in natural ecosystems. Some states now ban the sale and propagation of burning bush due to its invasiveness.

ASIAN BITTERSWEET (*Celastrus orbiculatus*)
Native to China, Japan, and Korea, Asian bittersweet was introduced to North America in the 1860s as a hardy and attractive ornamental. The woody vine has since escaped cultivation to colonize many natural areas, where it can climb up to 90 feet, twining around and strangling fully grown trees. Asian bittersweet can also choke out understory native plants with its dense foliage. It's readily spread through root growth and by birds that feast on the bright red berries throughout the winter. Yellow capsules open to reveal bright red berries in the fall, making the vine a popular choice for wreath-making.

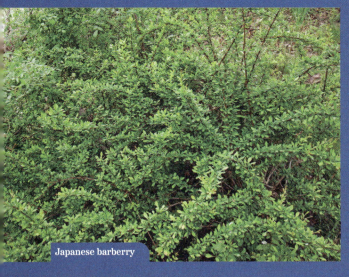

Japanese barberry

For many years, purple loosestrife was sold as an ornamental plant.

Norway maple

Burning bush

Asian bittersweet can kill a fully grown tree by girdling its trunk.

Asian bittersweet berries

IN IT FOR THE LONG HAUL

A soil seed bank is a collection of seeds that are dormant in the soil. Invasive plant seeds can remain viable in the soil seed bank for many years, lying in wait for the perfect combination of moisture, temperature, and light to sprout. Even if you remove all the visible invasive plants from an area, those pesky seeds can continue sprouting new plants for years to come. This means that successful control of invasive species requires a long-term approach. But just how long term are we talking? While some invasive plant seeds, like garlic mustard, can remain viable for up to 10 years, others, like multiflora rose, can lurk in the soil for up to two decades. So, what can you do to prevent these pesky seedbanks from causing trouble? The best approach is to prevent the introduction of invasive plant species in the first place. By being mindful of the plants you bring into your garden, you can prevent the establishment of new seedbanks. If you do find yourself dealing with invasive plants and their persistent seeds, be sure to take a long-term management approach that accounts for the soil seed bank. As you remove invasive plants, fill the vacant spots with native plants, and continue to observe and dig out any newly sprouted invasives as they appear.

Use a chainsaw or handsaw to cut and remove woody, invasive plants like honeysuckle. ↗

it's important to use this method with caution. Always be sure to clean equipment after use to avoid transporting invasive plant seeds or fragments from one area to another.

CULTURAL CONTROL

Cultural control methods involve changing the conditions in the landscape to prevent the spread of invasive plants and make your yard less hospitable for them. This can include practices such as planting native species and ensuring proper sanitation of lawncare equipment so you're not inadvertently transporting seeds or plant materials from one area to another. It can also include checking yourself and your pets for stray plant seeds when out hiking so you don't bring any plants back home with you.

Using a boot brush to remove dirt and debris in which plant seeds might be lurking is also a good idea after a hike. While cultural control methods may not completely eradicate invasive plants, they can help prevent the spread of problem plants and reduce their impact on the environment.

CHEMICAL CONTROL

Chemical control methods involve using herbicides to kill invasive plants. It might be hard to stomach the thought of using herbicides in the wildlife garden, but they are sometimes warranted when trying to control aggressive plants and when other means of removal have failed to eradicate problem species. Herbicides should always be used with careful planning and adherence to safety protocols to ensure that the treatment achieves the desired results without causing unintended harm to your garden. When used responsibly and in conjunction with other control methods, such as mechanical and cultural approaches, chemical control can be a valuable tool in the broader effort to combat invasive plants and protect nearby habitats. Always use

FROM TOP
Be sure to check pets after hiking in natural areas to ensure that you're not carrying home any stray seeds.

Use a boot brush to clean mud and debris from your shoes before leaving an area where there are known invasive plants.

DANDELIONS: INVASIVE OR NOT?

Ah, the dandelion, a weed that inspires both love and hate among gardeners and homeowners. Despite their reputation, dandelions are not actually invasive in the United States because they only thrive in cultivated landscapes and do not pose a threat to native plants or wildlife. Brought to the Americas by European colonists, dandelions are native to Eurasia. Due to their ability to thrive in disturbed areas and to spread quickly through wind-blown seeds, dandelions can quickly take over a lawn, leading many homeowners to view them as a nuisance. But the bright yellow flowers actually provide some important ecological benefits. They provide a source of pollen and nectar for pollinators, especially in areas barren of native flowering plants. And their deep taproots help to break up compacted soil, making them particularly useful in areas prone to poor soil conditions. Whether you view dandelions as a welcome addition to otherwise boring monocultures of grass or as a nuisance, if you do decide to remove them from your lawn or garden, remember to do so in an eco-friendly way that avoids the use of harmful chemicals.

While dandelions are non-native in the United States, plenty of pollinators, like this hover fly, enjoy collecting nectar from their blooms.

herbicides responsibly and in accordance with the manufacturer's label (it's the law!) and avoid using them in areas where they may drift onto non-target plants.

Dispose of Plants Responsibly

Because invasive plants can spread through the unintentional release of seeds or plants parts, which can then take root and grow in natural areas, it's essential to properly dispose of all plant parts once removed. Many plants can be securely bagged, baked in the sun for a few weeks to effectively kill all plant parts, and disposed of in the trash. Avoid composting invasive plants that spread vegetatively or plants with fruits or seeds, as home compost piles generally don't reach high enough temperatures to effectively kill all plant parts. For large woody species that don't reproduce vegetatively, you can use a chipper to create mulch, which can be used in the garden so long as fruits and seeds are not present. If you have a large amount of invasive plant material to dispose of, you may need to contact your local waste management facility to find out if there are special disposal procedures in place. Some areas have specific regulations for the disposal of invasive species, and it is important to follow these regulations to prevent future invasions.

Volunteer

Volunteering with local conservation organizations can be a fun and rewarding way to help control invasive plants in your local community. Many organizations offer training sessions and workshops that provide volunteers with the knowledge and tools they need to manage invasive plants. By learning firsthand from the professionals, you can feel more empowered in your own efforts to control invasive species in your home landscape. Volunteering with local conservation organizations will also encourage you to meet like-minded individuals who share your passion for conservation while lending the planet—and your local flora and fauna—a helping hand.

Volunteering to remove invasive plants from a local park is a great way to learn about plant identification and management methods from experts.

Chapter 5

LEAVE YOUR LEAVES

From the feathery fronds of ferns to the sturdier stalks of an oak, leaves create the foundation of many healthy habitats. If you're fortunate enough to have large trees in your yard, leaves can help create healthy habitats at home too, but only if you let them. Unfortunately, homeowners and landscapers often view leaves as problematic, raking and disposing of them almost as quickly as they fall. This practice of leaf removal, however, has big consequences for people and wildlife alike.

Why Leaves Matter

Plants form the base of food webs in nearly every ecosystem on the planet. Through photosynthesis, plants absorb sunlight through chlorophyll stored in their leaves. By taking in sunlight, along with water and carbon dioxide, they create chemical energy known as glucose. This energy is then transferred throughout the entire ecosystem when animals eat plants, or when animals eat other animals that eat plants. The process of photosynthesis also results in the production and release of oxygen. In other words, we can thank leaves for sustaining life on Earth. And if you think that leaves have served their purpose once they've fallen from the treetops, think again. Leaves are the type of gift that keeps on giving.

Nutrient Recycling

Fallen leaves play an important role in the carbon cycle and in nutrient recycling. They absorb carbon dioxide from the atmosphere during photosynthesis, and when they fall to the ground and begin to break down, they release that carbon back into the soil. They also release small amounts of essential macronutrients like nitrogen, phosphorus, and potassium, which are fundamental to plant growth. Plants use nitrogen to grow healthy leaves and produce chlorophyll, which gives leaves their green color. Phosphorus helps plants form new roots and produce seeds, flowers, and fruit. And potassium is important for stem growth and strength. Removing leaves from the landscape removes all those wonderful nutrients that both replenish the soil and are vital for plant growth. It also creates the need to replace those nutrients in your lawn. For many homeowners, this means dousing the lawn each spring with synthetic fertilizers that often end up in nearby waterways and contribute to issues like harmful algal blooms.

Habitat

Fallen leaves, twigs, needles, and other bits and pieces of vegetation on the forest floor combine to create the duff layer, a blanket of organic material that is several inches thick. Over time, insects and other arthropods, like springtails, help break down organic matter in this layer of leaf litter before it's further decomposed by fungi and bacteria. As you walk through the forest, you might not think much of this spongy layer of slowly decomposing organic matter. But peel back those layers of leaves, and you'll discover a micro habitat filled with millions of organisms living in harmony to keep the forest healthy.

Leaf litter is teeming with microscopic organisms, but it also supports an array of other wildlife, including insects, birds, and small

TOP
Throughout the growing season, leaves provide shade and food for a diversity of wildlife.

....

BOTTOM LEFT
After falling, leaves continue offering critical habitat for critters looking for a safe place to overwinter.

....

BOTTOM RIGHT
Wolf spiders are among the many types of wildlife that rely on leaf litter.

....

WHY LEAVES CHANGE COLOR

Each autumn, as days grow shorter, trees begin the process of shedding their leaves. First, chlorophyll production starts to slow, eventually stopping entirely. Chlorophyll does not absorb green wavelengths, but instead reflects green light, which gives leaves their green color. When chlorophyll production stops, the carotenoids and anthocyanin in leaves are unmasked, making way for one of nature's best spectacles—fall colors.

After a few fleeting weeks of fiery hues, the landscape dulls to shades of brown as leaves tumble to the ground, at least for those far enough away from the equator to experience this seasonal change. With colder temperatures on the way and water becoming scarcer throughout the winter months, trees begin to conserve energy by directing nutrients below ground. With no leaves to capture the sun's energy, deciduous trees stop photosynthesizing during the chilly winter months. Evergreen trees that retain their needles continue to photosynthesize so long as they have enough water to grow in wintery conditions. While some might look at winter as dreary and depressing (hello, seasonal affective disorder), life in the leaf litter is hard at work preparing for the season ahead.

mammals that rely on leaves for food and shelter. Luna moths, for example, use fallen leaves to create a cozy cocoon that protects them from predators and dropping temperatures as they overwinter. Woolly bear caterpillars also spend their winters safely tucked in the leaf litter. And ground-foraging birds like turkeys, pheasants, and doves root through this leafy layer in search of food like insects, seeds, and nuts.

Other Ecosystem Services

In addition to helping with nutrient recycling and providing wildlife habitat, leaves contribute to a range of other ecosystem services, like

forming a protective layer that helps reduce soil erosion and increase water retention. For insects like fireflies, this is crucial. Fireflies spend the majority of their lives as larvae living in the leaf litter or underground where they feed on slugs, snails, and other soft-bodied arthropods. Leaves insulate soil, keeping it from drying out and providing temperature control for a range of ground-dwelling critters. This layer of organic material also bolsters water quality by creating a natural filter that traps pollution like sediments and nutrients before they flow into streams, rivers, and lakes.

Don't Be a Leaf Thief

On the surface, fallen leaves may seem like nature's waste. After all, yard waste like leaves accounts for around 35 million tons of annual municipal solid waste every year. But leaf litter is anything but waste. If you have trees in your yard, you should have leaf litter. Learning to manage leaves in ways that are beneficial to nature while aligning with your neighborhood's expectations, however, may take a bit of work.

Let Leaves Lie

Lazy landscapers rejoice, because the very best way to manage leaves in a wildlife garden is to not manage them at all. Leaving your leaves where they fall and letting them naturally decompose is a wonderful way of supporting ecosystem services at home. Over time, leaves naturally decompose, creating a layer of rich leaf litter that will support a diversity of wildlife, create healthier soils, and support plants by recycling nutrients back into the soil. Leaving leaves where they fall also ensures that any critters that might

Leaves provide important habitat for fireflies. ↑

Installing a "Leave the Leaves" sign in your garden can help educate neighbors about the intent of your landscape. →

be hunkered down for the winter ahead are not disturbed. But leaving the leaves might not be an option for everyone. Some communities mandate leaf cleanups, forcing homeowners to face fines for not maintaining tidy landscapes. And other homeowners simply prefer a more orderly yard. Thankfully, you can keep things neat while still raking in all the benefits that fallen leaves have to offer.

Make with the Rake

Can't leave the leaves? Then grab a rake. If your leaves must be moved, raking is the most sustainable alternative to letting them overwinter where they fall. And raking has many benefits. For starters, creating giant leaf piles to jump into is one of the greatest treats of autumn. More than that, raking can also help to ensure that leaves don't suffocate grass and other landscape plants. Those with just a few small trees can rake leaves into nearby garden beds. As the leaves decompose, they'll help replenish the soil, giving your plants a little boost. If you have larger trees that drop an abundance of leaves, consider mimicking the forest by creating dedicated garden beds under the tree canopy where leaves can be safely stowed each year. Plant a variety of shade-loving and fruit-bearing native plants in these understory gardens that will provide birds and other wildlife with food for winter, and you'll have yourself a lovely little forest habitat in no time.

When you rake leaves into garden beds, they can be left to naturally decompose from one year to the next, or they can be composted in the spring once critters have emerged from their leafy overwintering habitat. If you opt to compost, rake leaves out of the garden beds in the spring and shred them using a lawn mower or leaf shredder. While shredding isn't necessary, it will help leaves decompose a bit quicker. If leaves must be taken off property, send them to a good home. Many cities offer leaf pickup programs where leaves are collected and transported to local landscapers to be used as mulch. This is a better choice than having the garbage truck pick up plastic bags full of leaves to be carried off to the dump.

Leave the Leaf Blower Behind

Leaf blowers may make quick work of leaf cleanup, but they also have harmful impacts for people and wildlife. The roar of a leaf blower can grow as loud as a jet engine, reaching a whopping 120 decibels. This noise pollution can disrupt both human and animal communities, causing stress and even hearing loss. Gas-powered leaf blowers also spew harmful pollutants like carbon monoxide, nitrogen oxides, and particulate matter into the air. One study from 2011 found that a consumer-grade leaf blower can emit

TOP LEFT
When raking leaves, be sure to leave time for play.
....

TOP RIGHT
Gas-powered leaf blowers are one of the heaviest carbon-emitting lawn care tools.
....

BOTTOM LEFT
Curb your carbon by opting for a rake.
....

BOTTOM RIGHT
Consider creating dedicated garden beds for leaves.
....

more pollutants than a pickup truck, making leaf blowers a bad choice for the wildlife garden. If you must use one, opt for an electric blower that will at least reduce carbon emissions compared to their gas-powered counterparts.

To Mulch or Not to Mulch?

Leaf mulching may sound like a great idea for those who worry that leaving their leaves where they fall will suffocate their grass (spoiler alert, it might!). Leaf mulching usually means running over your leaves with a lawn mower once or twice to shred them into smaller pieces that will more easily break down throughout the winter months. Shredding your leaves will certainly accelerate the time it takes for leaves to break down and it can help prevent the suffocation of turfgrass (if you're still into that sort of thing). But—and this is a big *but*— it also kills many of the beautiful and wonderful creatures that have hunkered down in the leaf litter looking for a warm and cozy home for the winter. If you're hoping to help wildlife, it's best to skip leaf mulching. If you're really worried about turfgrass, rake the leaves off of the lawn and into a dedicated compost pile or garden bed.

BE A GOOD NEIGHBOR

Raking might be more environmentally friendly than leaf blowing, but it can also be hard work, especially for older adults or those unable to participate in manual labor. Helping your neighbors with this fall chore can make their lives a little easier while strengthening community bonds. It also helps foster community sustainability by lessening the need for leaf blowers. Next time you're faced with fall leaf cleanup, host a community-wide raking event, or simply offer to rake a neighbor's yard (or entice your kids to help out in exchange for a sweet treat).

Watch for Storm Drain Clogs

Leaves are great for wildlife but leaving the leaves can have unintended consequences for the community. Leaves and other debris like twigs can clog storm drains when not properly contained, which can lead to flooding and drainage backups. This is especially important after heavy rain or snowfall events. To prevent clogs, keep an eye on storm drains in your neighborhood. If you spot a clog, use a rake to remove and properly dispose of (or compost) the debris.

FROM LEFT
Many animals, like snakes, overwinter in leaf litter.

Be sure to keep your storm drains clear of debris.

Chapter 6

GO WILD FOR WILDLIFE

For people, gardens are places of beauty and tranquility. For wildlife, however, they can be quite the opposite. Stripped bare of native plants that provide food and shelter and doused in chemicals that dissuade visitation by wild neighbors, many gardens have been rendered ecologically sterile. These spaces that provide joy and wonder for people must also be sanctuaries for wildlife. As you begin your journey toward creating an oasis for wildlife at home, examine your relationship with wild animals. Animals have been a part of the landscape long before humans and it's worth considering how reshaping your relationship with them can foster a more nature-friendly garden.

Supporting Wildlife in the Garden

Animals need four basic things to thrive: food, water, shelter, and safe places to raise their young. By being thoughtful about the design of your landscape, you can provide all of these things. Nectar-rich flowers support pollinators, and berry bushes provide food for birds and a diversity of mammals. Small ponds, birdbaths, or puddling stations can help wildlife quench their thirst on a hot summer day, while trees, brush piles, and nesting boxes can provide

Eastern chipmunk

Gray treefrog ↑

Crab spider →

homes and shelter for wildlife and safe places to nest.

Gardening for wildlife may require retraining your mind to see beauty in different ways. Where an ornamental rose garden may be desirable to some, landscapes that create habitats for plants and wildlife while supporting natural cycles of nutrient and water recycling become the new marker of beauty in the wildlife garden. This means finding beauty in function over form, which often requires a tolerance for imperfection.

Rethink the Purpose of Plants

Plants first appeared on the land around 500 million years ago, paving the way for the emergence of animals that depend on them for food and shelter. As humans began to reshape the landscape for their own aesthetic tastes, the practice of using plants purely as decoration began to emerge. While there is nothing inherently wrong with appreciating the beauty of plants, we mustn't forget that they serve ecological roles beyond appearance alone. Animals evolved to eat plants. Even carnivores rely on healthy populations of plants as a food source for their prey. Unfortunately, nibbled leaves might not always jibe with your gardening goals.

Gardeners often strive for perfect plants, hoping that every stem, leaf, and bloom remains pristine and untouched. But by allowing insects like caterpillars to nibble on your plants, you're helping to support an entire food chain. Many terrestrial birds feed their young a diet of almost exclusively insects, which rely on plants for their own survival. It may be frustrating to see

your carefully tended plants nipped and nibbled by wildlife, but these animals are simply trying to survive in a world made ever more inhospitable to them at the hands of human development.

Supporting wildlife means increasing your tolerance for imperfection and rejoicing at the sight of holes in leaves, for this means the garden served its purpose in feeding someone or something. Nibbled leaves are a natural part of a healthy ecosystem. In fact, many plants

↑ A cardinal visits a birdbath for a sip of fresh water.

← Many mammals, like this eastern cottontail rabbit, are considered pests, but it's important to remember that they need food as much as the beloved bees and butterflies that we welcome into the garden.

Finding injured or abandoned wildlife in your yard can be troubling, but attempting to handle or care for injured wildlife on your own can often cause more harm than good. If you come across injured wildlife or animals in distress, it's best to contact a local wildlife rehabilitation center for guidance and assistance. Trained professionals have the expertise and resources needed to assess the situation, provide proper care, and release the animal back into its natural habitat once it has recovered.

Keep in mind that finding young animals in your yard is not always cause for concern. Fawns, for example, are often left hidden in tall grass by their mothers while they forage for food. This behavior is a natural survival strategy to protect young deer from potential predators. Finding a fawn alone does not necessarily mean it's abandoned or in danger, so it's best to observe from a distance and check on the fawn periodically to ensure its mother returns.

· ·

Female deer often leave their fawns hidden in tall grass while they forage.

evolved to withstand a certain level of grazing or browsing from animals. By planting a wide diversity and abundance of native plants that are adapted to your local ecoregion, you'll reduce the likelihood of damage from these animals by giving them plenty to feast on.

While sawfly larvae can create unsightly holes in leaves, they provide food for a variety of critters, including birds and amphibians.

· ·

DIY Projects to Help Wildlife

Planting native plants is essential for supporting wildlife. In many urban and suburban landscapes, however, wildlife benefit from an extra helping hand. This means providing human-made resources that will help to support wildlife while you (and hopefully your neighbors) work to restore ecosystem function in your community. There are many DIY projects that will aid in supporting critters in the garden. Here are a few ideas to get you started.

Create a Butterfly Puddling Station

Butterflies spend sunny afternoons flitting from flower to flower in search of nectar, but many species are also drawn to damp areas where they extract essential nutrients, including salts and minerals. It's not unusual to see groups of butterflies huddling around a mud puddle or even a dung pile, engaging in this practice known as puddling. You can create your own puddling station in the garden to support butterflies in search of essential nutrients by filling a small dish or birdbath with damp sand, compost, manure, or mud and placing a few perching stones, like river rocks or gravel, in the mixture. Position the puddling station near nectar-rich flowering plants, and remoisten the mixture often, especially on hot sunny days when the station will be prone to drying out. Create a similar water station for other pollinators, like bees and wasps, by filling a shallow dish with water and perching stones. You may even be surprised to see birds using the water station once in a while. Be sure to replace the water frequently to prevent your water station from becoming a breeding ground for mosquitos.

Build a Brush Pile

A thriving wildlife garden will see both predators and prey. It's a beautiful thing we call the circle of life. And while it's natural—maybe even exciting—to see nature play out in your yard, it's also important to offer sanctuary for small critters so your garden doesn't become a buffet for larger predators. Small animals will benefit from safe spaces where they can go to escape the jaws and claws of hungry predators. Dense shrubs and trees provide important cover for a variety of wildlife, but you can also create brush piles where chipmunks, rabbits, squirrels, birds, and other small creatures can find shelter when needed.

A brush pile is a deliberately arranged stack of branches, twigs, and woody debris created to provide protection from predators. The piles can also serve as nesting and foraging sites for a variety of animals. To build one, find an inconspicuous spot in your landscape away from your home to deter wildlife from nesting or burrowing too close to your home's foundation. Collect fallen branches, twigs, and logs of various sizes and position a base layer of larger logs to create a stable foundation. Next, stack smaller branches, leaves, and plant trimmings

on top. Include a mix of deciduous and evergreen materials to accommodate different wildlife preferences and consider adding hollow plant stems to create natural cavities for solitary nesting bees. As the brush pile decomposes over time, be sure to add new natural materials to maintain the structure's integrity so that it continues providing a safe haven for wildlife.

CLOCKWISE
Creating a brush pile can be as simple as stacking various sizes of sticks and branches in an inconspicuous spot in your yard.

You can create a more intentional brush pile by strategically placing larger logs at the bottom to create plenty of open spaces for wildlife to hide.

Providing cover will help small wildlife find protection from predators like this red-tailed hawk.

Make a Toad Abode

Toads are often overlooked visitors in the wildlife garden, but they play an important role in controlling pest populations. You can help support toads by building a simple toad adobe where they can escape from predators like raccoons and birds of prey. Start by selecting a shady and humid area of your garden, preferably near vegetation and a water source. Using natural and non-toxic materials like rocks, logs, or clay pots, build a small shelter with a partially buried entrance to mimic a toad's natural habitat. Ensure the structure is well insulated and provides protection from predators. Add a layer of damp soil or leaves inside the toad house to create a cool and humid environment. Because amphibians like toads, frogs, and salamanders are sensitive to environmental changes, their presence in your garden can be an indicator of overall ecosystem health, so check on your toad abode often for evidence of a new resident.

This toad abode was made by chipping a small opening out of a terra cotta pot and sanding sharp edges to create a smooth entrance.

Hang a Pinecone Feeder

Like leaves, pinecones can be left to naturally decompose where they fall. But they may not be favored by gardeners wishing to maintain a tidy appearance in the wildlife garden. Before tossing or composting your conifer cones, consider putting them to good use by crafting DIY bird feeders. Start by collecting untreated and natural pinecones from pesticide-free gardens. Using a butter knife or spatula, spread peanut butter over the scales of the pinecone. It's best to use organic unsalted, unsweetened peanut butter that's free from additives. If peanut allergies are a concern, opt for an alternative like sunflower seed butter instead. Once they're coated in peanut butter, roll the pinecones in a mixture of birdseed and leave to dry for several days, allowing the feeders to harden. Once dry, hang feeders securely in your garden with natural twine or string and enjoy observing the birds that stop by for a taste.

Hang your pinecone feeder in an area of your yard where birds are likely to visit.

Wildlife Pond in a Weekend

Installing a small pond in your garden is a great way to attract a diversity of wildlife. While the project may sound daunting, it can be managed in just a single weekend, especially if you opt to use a pre-formed pond liner, which you can find at your local home improvement store or garden center. Here's a step-by-step guide to get you started:

Prepare Your Site Begin by choosing a location in yard that receives a good balance of sunlight and shade. Dappled sunlight is best as it promotes aquatic plant growth, which will ensure your pond maintains appropriate levels of oxygen for aquatic wildlife. Clear the area of any debris, rocks, or roots, and level the ground where the pond will be placed. This step is crucial to create a stable foundation and prevent any stress on the pond liner, which could cause cracking and leakage.

Select a Pond Liner When deciding on a pre-formed pond liner, consider your preferred size and shape. Some liners are round, while others mimic a more natural curve. Also consider whether you'd like to install a multi-tiered pond with a waterfall. In this case, you can buy a pond kit that includes a waterfall

filter or spillway that pumps water from a lower basin up to a rocky ledge or streambed where it can naturally cascade back down into the pond. Whatever you choose, the liner should be made of durable, weather-resistant material designed to withstand outdoor conditions and the weight of water once filled. As an alternative to a pre-formed pond liner, you can opt for a large sheet made from a material like PVC, which will give you more flexibility in your pond depth and design.

Dig and Install Carefully dig a hole that matches your pond liner's shape and dimensions. If you're using a plastic sheet, you'll have flexibility in how wide and deep you dig your hole. The depth of the pond can vary but should typically be a minimum of 18 inches to provide habitat for various wildlife. Ensure that the pond's edges are level and stable by

FROM TOP
Create places for birds to perch and safety ramps for wildlife to escape your pond in case they fall into the water.

Use your pond liner to mark your area for digging.

Filling your pond liner with a thin layer of gravel or stone can prevent shifting.

adding a shallow layer of sand to the bottom of the hole. Once the hole is ready, carefully place the pond liner into it, making sure it sits firmly and evenly. To prevent the liner from shifting, backfill around the edges with sand or soil.

Choose the Right Pump Selecting an appropriate pump is essential for maintaining water circulation and preventing stagnation, which could deter wildlife from using your pond. The pump you choose should be sized according to the volume of water it needs to circulate. A good rule of thumb is to circulate the entire pond volume at least once every hour. Be mindful of the pump's energy consumption and opt for an energy-efficient model if possible. Adding a small fountain will enhance the visual appeal and oxygenation of the pond and attract an array of species, including birds, which are drawn to the sound of moving water.

Add Hardscaping and Landscaping Once your pond is firmly in place, you can begin adding special touches. Surround the pond's perimeter with a border of stones, pebbles, or decorative bricks. These materials also serve to anchor the liner, prevent soil erosion, and provide a stable surface for plants or ornamental features. Planting aquatic vegetation both in and around your pond, including native water lilies, cattails, and irises, will also provide shelter and food sources for visiting wildlife.

Construct Perches and Safety Ramps To make your pond more inviting to birds and other critters, add perches by stacking flat rocks or bricks in the pond. The top of your perch should be high enough that it barely grazes the surface of the water. Birds will use these perches to land and take off while drinking or bathing. Also position bird-friendly plants, such as shrubs

TREE SNAGS

When left standing, dead trees, also called snags, provide habitat for an array of species. Nuthatches and woodpeckers, for instance, enjoy pecking insects from dead and decaying wood, while raccoons, opossums, and flying squirrels will use cavities for nesting. Snags can also provide great lookouts for raptors like owls, hawks, and eagles. If you have a dead tree in your yard, it's best to leave it for wildlife, so long as it does not pose a safety risk to your home or community if it were to unexpectedly fall.

A juvenile tree swallow waits for its parents to return to the nest with food.

and trees, nearby to offer both perches and cover from predators. For other wildlife like frogs, toads, or small mammals that might accidentally fall into the pond, install safety ramps. These can be made from various materials, such as rocks, logs, or wooden planks that gently slope upwards out of the water, offering an escape route for animals should they fall into the pond.

Chapter 7

BEE FRIENDLY

Love 'em or hate 'em, bees are critical to the health of the planet. A world without bees and their pollinating kin would mean a world with desolate dinner plates and barren backyards. Nearly 80 percent of the world's flowering plants, including 87 of the world's leading food crops, rely on animal pollination to some degree. Without this critical ecosystem service, we could kiss some of our favorite foods goodbye, including apples, bananas, blueberries, pumpkins, pears, peaches, cherries, raspberries, blackberries, strawberries, watermelon, and (most important) coffee and chocolate.

A Bit about Bees

Bees are in the order Hymenoptera, which also includes wasps and ants, and there is an uncanny resemblance between the three insect groups. Bees descended from wasps around 125 million years ago after some wasps developed vegetarian lifestyles and began gathering pollen rather than prey. But wasps aren't even our first pollinators. Fossil records suggest that beetles and flies evolved to pollinate flowers first.

All told, there are more than 20,000 species of bees in the world, and around 4000 species are native to the United States. While humid tropical regions are often touted as supporting the greatest insect biodiversity, native bee

HAULIN' POLLEN

. . . .

When it comes to pollinators, bees seem to always hog the spotlight, and for good reason. While they aren't the only animal pollinators, bees have developed specialized behavioral and physical traits that make them our most efficient pollinators. During the day, bees forage on flowers to collect nectar (their primary energy source) and pollen (their primary protein source). As they forage, their specialized branched or feathered body hairs help pick up pollen, which is then delivered to the next bloom the bee visits.

Both male and female bees feed on nectar, but only females gather pollen, which they bring back to the nest to feed their offspring. Bees and other pollinators do not collect pollen with the intent of helping plants reproduce. Instead, pollination is a byproduct of animals collecting food for themselves and for their offspring. Over evolutionary time, plants began to develop floral rewards like nectar to attract animals to their blooms, bringing big benefits to the bees and blooms alike.

. . . .

Bees are efficient pollinators thanks to their hairy bodies, which are great for picking up pollen as they visit flowers.

diversity is greatest in warm, temperate dry regions of the world, like the deserts of California, Nevada, Utah, Arizona, and New Mexico, which offer ideal environmental conditions for ground-nesting bees. With 70 percent of native bees in the United States nesting in the ground, it's no surprise that these desert landscapes boast some of the highest concentrations of bee diversity anywhere in world.

While some bees are small and shiny, others are large and hairy. Some are bright and colorful while others don muted shades of brown and black. And while some enjoy social lifestyles, others prefer to spend their days alone. Identifying the various bees that call your garden home is essential to better understanding how to support them throughout their varied lifecycles. Here are a few notable groups of bees you might find in your garden.

→ → → → → → → → → → → → → → → →

Mason Bees

Mason bees are most common in the western United States, with only 27 of North America's 150 species living east of the Mississippi. These bees range in size from 0.2 to 0.8 inches, and most are metallic in coloration with many wearing bright hues of green and blue. All females are solitary and fertile, building nests in cavities found in dead wood or hollow plant stems. Mason bees sometimes construct nests in artificial sites too, like bundled bamboo or wood blocks with drilled cavities, using mud to build walls between brood cells in nests.

Leafcutter Bees

Leafcutter bees are medium to large bees that range in size from 0.4 to 0.8 inches. They have stout black bodies and flattened abdomens that have bands of pale hairs on top and long hairs underneath called *scopa*. While most bees carry pollen on their legs, leafcutter bees carry pollen on the undersides of their abdomens, making them appear bright yellow or gold after a day of visiting blooms. All species are solitary, constructing nests in existing cavities, like hollow plant stems or abandoned beetle tunnels. Leafcutter bees construct their nests with pieces of leaves or flower petals that they cut with their strong mandibles. But don't worry—the circular holes that they cut from leaves and flowers cause only cosmetic damage and should not be cause for concern but rather a welcome sign of this pollinator's presence in your garden.

Sweat Bees

Sweat bees are perhaps most well known for their showy metallic colors, but most species in this family wear less conspicuous black or brown attire. Sweat bees can be quite tiny, with the smallest species growing to only a few millimeters in length. These bees are so named for their attraction to perspiration, which you may have discovered when out weeding the garden. Nesting behavior varies among species, but most are ground nesters. Others prefer to nest in rotting wood. As for social behavior, many sweat bees are solitary, but some are semi-social and others nest communally.

Honey Bees

Characterized by fuzzy bodies and black-and-yellow-striped abdomens, honey bees exhibit highly organized social nesting behavior, constructing hives where a complex hierarchy of worker bees, drones, and a queen work collaboratively to forage, nurse, and maintain the colony. They are important pollinators of many crops, and like other bee species, they've been plagued by population decline caused by pests, diseases, and pesticide exposure. But before jumping into beekeeping, it's important to understand that honey bees are non-native in the United States and can outcompete native bees for pollen and nectar, especially when present in large numbers. If you want to help native pollinators, it's best to plant a variety of native flowering plants and create habitats that will support them.

Long-horned Bees

Long-horned bees are small to medium bees that range in size from 0.3 to 0.7 inches. They have robust and hairy bodies, conspicuously hairy hind legs, and most species have namesake long antennae. While many long-horned bees have a foraging preference for Asteraceae

species, including sunflowers, asters, and daisies, others are considered generalists and forage on a diversity of flowering plants. All long-horned bees nest in the ground, where they construct and provision individual brood cells for their offspring.

Bumble Bees

Bumble bees are large and robust bees with hairy bodies and bands of hairs that vary in coloration from yellow, orange, white, or black to brown depending on the species. Unlike most bees that collect dry pollen, bumble bees (like honey bees) moisten pollen with nectar to make it sticky before packing it into the hairs on their hindlegs, called pollen baskets, or *corbicula*. While many native bees are solitary, bumble bees are social insects, nesting in colonies underground or in human-made structures like abandoned birdhouses. Each fall, most of the bumble bees in a colony die, leaving mated queen bees to hibernate over the winter. In the spring, large queen bumble bees emerge from their winter slumber to begin foraging and building a new colony. Once she successfully rears her first brood, the new workers will take over foraging duties, leaving the queen to lay eggs as she continues to grow her colony.

Squash Bees

As their name suggests, squash bees are specialists, pollinating only members of the cucurbit family, including cucumbers, pumpkins, squash, watermelon, and zucchini. Squash bees are about the size of honey bees, but unlike their honey-producing cousins, lead solitary lives. Squash blossoms invite pollinators to visit during early morning hours before midday heat forces the blooms to shrivel shut. Unmated females will join males for an afternoon nap inside the shriveled squash blooms, while mated females spend their afternoons constructing underground nests. Take a peek inside a squash flower at midday and you might be surprised to discover some snoozing bees.

Carpenter Bees

Carpenter bees are large, mostly black bees that nest by tunneling into wood, bamboo, or dead plant stalks. In natural areas, carpenter bees prefer constructing nests in soft woods and dead and decaying trees and logs. In suburban and urban areas, they may bore into wooden decks or furniture. When present in small numbers, they generally do not cause structural damage. Their larvae, however, can attract other predators like woodpeckers in search of a snack, which can be problematic and warrant control measures.

OPPOSITE, CLOCKWISE
FROM TOP LEFT
Mason Bee

....

Leafcutter bee

....

Honey bee

....

Bumble bee

....

Long-horned bee

....

Sweat bee

....

THIS PAGE
Squash bee

....

A CASE OF MISTAKEN IDENTITY

· ·

Due to similarities in size and coloration, bumble bees and carpenter bees are often mistaken for one another. Need a sure way to tell the difference? Carpenter bees generally have a shiny heinie, where bumble bees have a hairier derriere.

· ·

The abdomen of bumble bees (top) tends to be hairy. The abdomen of carpenter bees (bottom) tends to be hairless and shiny.

Other Insect Pollinators

Bees are certainly some of our most important pollinators, but there are other wildlife groups that deserve a share of the spotlight too. From butterflies and moths to flies and wasps, here are a few additional pollinator groups we can thank for keeping our world abloom.

Butterflies and Moths

Butterflies spend their days flitting from flower to flower in search of sweet nectar. Their long thin legs keep them perched above blooms, making them less efficient pollinators than bees. Nevertheless, as they visit flowers, they pick up pollen that is then transported to the next blossom they visit. When the sun goes down, butterflies rest while their nocturnal brethren—moths—awake to take the night shift of pollination. Where butterflies are generally attracted to brightly colored flowers, moths fancy paler blooms. Some plants, like the yucca, are exclusively pollinated by moths.

Flies

The world's nearly 125,000 species of flies bring many benefits to our gardens and surrounding habitats. Some of these benefits include predation, decomposition, parasitism, and you guessed it—pollination. Like bees, flies feed on nectar and pollen. But unlike bees, which have excellent maternal instincts and bring pollen back to the nest for offspring, most flies don't exhibit maternal care, instead carrying the extra pollen to the next blossom they visit.

Beetles

Beetles represent a staggering 40 percent of all known insects in the world. Beetles evolved to pollinate ancient plants, including magnolias, in the absence of other pollinators, like bees and butterflies, which hadn't yet emerged on the pollination scene. Today, beetles are important pollinators for native plants including pawpaw, tulip tree, sweetshrub, and water lilies. Other native plants that benefit from beetle pollination include goldenrod, spirea, spicebush, sunflower, and yarrow.

Wasps

Wasps are important pollinators, but the benefits they provide in the garden don't stop there. In fact, wasps are perhaps most important for pest control. Adults generally feed on nectar, but they prey on insects and spiders, which they bring back to the nest to feed to their larval young. And many wasps are parasitoids, laying eggs in or on other organisms, ultimately killing the host.

CLOCKWISE
Eastern tiger swallowtail butterfly

Bee fly

Paper wasp

Locust borer beetle

TO BEE OR NOT TO BEE?

. . . .

Bee-lieve it or not, many insects mimic bees to avoid predation. Hover flies are excellent bee mimics and are often mistakenly called "sweat bees" despite being flies. So how can you tell the difference? Bees have two pairs of wings and flies have just one. Despite their cheeky disguise, hover flies are great pollinators, and many species have carnivorous larvae, making them wonderful beneficial insects to have in the garden.

. . . .

Hover flies are often mistaken for bees due to the black and yellow coloration of many species.

PREDATOR, PARASITE, OR PARASITOID?

. . . .

Confused about the difference between a predator, a parasite, and a parasitoid? Predators actively capture and eat prey, while parasites live in or on another organism, feeding at the expense of the host. While parasites generally do not kill their host, the life of a parasitoid is a bit more macabre. Adult parasitoids lay eggs in or on a host. Upon hatching, larval parasitoids feed and develop inside the body of the host, eventually killing it before emerging as an adult.

. . . .

Be a Friend to Bees

You can better support bees and other pollinators by planting more native flowering plants. Thanks to evolution, some species simply can't live without them. Pollinators can be broadly separated into two categories based on their foraging habits—specialists and generalists. Specialist bees have evolved to forage on specific plants (think squash bees, which only forage on plants in the cucurbit family). Generalists, however, are a bit less picky, foraging on a wider

variety of blooms, including non-native species. When native plants are replaced with non-native plants (or worse, invasive plants), pollinator specialists struggle to find food. It's like taking a toddler to a fancy restaurant—caviar simply won't do when the only thing they'll eat is mac and cheese. So, what's the solution? For starters, don't take toddlers to fancy restaurants. More important, provide pollinators with what they evolved to eat—native plants. But don't stop there. There are lots of other ways to create a bee-friendly landscape.

The Buzz about Lazy Landscaping

Filling your landscape with native plants will create the foundation that bees and other pollinators need to thrive. But there are lots of other landscape practices that will help to support them throughout their lifecycles, including adopting a lazier landscaping routine. If you think lazy landscaping is permission to throw your hands up and let your yard do whatever it likes, think again. Lazy landscaping means strategically reducing your carbon- and chemical-intensive inputs while allowing certain areas of your yard to grow and evolve without extensive intervention. This approach can promote the growth of habitat and floral resources for wildlife and save you time, energy, and money.

If you have a few bare spots in the yard, you can leave them for the bees. Ground-nesting bees need bare ground to find suitable underground habitat. If you don't have bare spots, then consider making some by clearing the vegetation from a few well-drained and sunny areas in your yard. It's best to select areas that don't get a lot of foot traffic to avoid conflicts with the bees you're hoping to attract. Also be sure to avoid creating bare spots on heavily

FROM LEFT
This native pollinator garden provides a variety of plants and nesting sites for bees and other pollinators.

Cellophane bees excavate small tunnels in sandy soils.

Leaves provide nesting sites for a variety of wildlife while insulating soil for ground-nesting bees and other underground organisms, so avoid clearing away all of your fallen leaves. ↑

. . . .

Cut stems provide ideal nesting sites for cavity nesting bees like mason bees and leafcutter bees. →

. . . .

sloped areas where the lack of vegetation may cause increased erosion.

Don't fret about garden cleanup either. Cavity-nesting bees need dead plant stems, especially those with hollow (or *pithy*) centers, to construct nests where they overwinter. Rather than removing dead plant stems during fall garden cleanup, leave the stems standing over winter. In spring, cut stems back at varying heights from 8 to 24 inches. This will provide open stems for bees to construct their nests and lay eggs. After hatching, larvae will spend the summer and fall growing and developing, overwintering in the stems and emerging as adults the following spring. You can remove the stems after the first few weeks of warm temperatures in the second spring when cavity nesting bees have emerged. Can't wait that long? Cut the stems at ground level and place them in a bundle somewhere safe in your yard. Need help remembering how long those plant stems should remain in the garden? Think of it this way: this year's flowers create next year's nests for the following year's bees.

Less frequent mowing can also support bees and pollinators by allowing lawn plants, like violets, clover, and dandelions, to flower, attracting more bees to your yard by providing the floral resources they need to forage. One study showed that mowing once every two weeks might be the sweet spot, finding that a two-week mowing interval attracted the highest bee abundance compared to one and three-week intervals (Lerman, 2018). While some of these lawn plants may not be native to your region, they can help to bridge the resource gap for hungry pollinators as you incorporate more native flowering plants into your landscape.

NO MOW MAY

No Mow May is an initiative born out of the United Kingdom that encourages homeowners and landowners to refrain from mowing their lawns during the month of May. The movement is meant to promote early blooms in the lawn that provide important floral resources for early pollinators to forage. Advocates of No Mow May tout the movement as an encouraging shift in perception of what a perfect lawn should look like, challenging the traditional notion that lawns require excessive maintenance and chemical inputs. But the movement is not without its faults.

Critics of the initiative note that the practice of infrequent mowing can encourage the establishment of undesirable species in the lawn, namely dandelions. The uncontrolled growth of grasses in the lawn can also encourage little critters like bunnies to nest in areas that will be mowed come June, leaving them homeless or worse.

No Mow May need not be an all-or-nothing initiative. You can simply reduce your frequency of mowing or consider keeping a small area of unmown lawn for pollinators to enjoy while tidying up the rest of your yard.

A WORD ON STINGS

Attracting bees and wasps to your home landscape may have you worried about increasing your risk of stings. Understanding how and why bees and wasps sting is an important first step in avoiding the risk. Stingers are a modification of an ovipositor, the egg-laying organ in insects, meaning only female bees and wasps are capable of stinging. You're more likely to be stung by a social wasp—like a paper wasp, yellowjacket, or hornet—or a honey bee, since these communal insects can be aggressively protective of their nests when disturbed. Unlike honey bees, wasps retain their stingers, and may sting multiple times. Solitary bees and wasps, which represent the majority of bee and wasp species, are less likely to sting and generally only attack when provoked. To avoid stings, be aware of your surroundings and always respect the space of wild animals. Avoid walking barefoot through your garden, especially in areas of known nests. Also avoid swatting, squishing, or otherwise harming bees and wasps unless absolutely necessary for personal safety.

As social insects, paper wasps can be aggressively protective of their nests but will generally not attack unless provoked.

← This bee house features nesting tubes and shelves that can be removed and cleaned each season.

↓ Bee houses with irreplaceable nesting cavities should be avoided.

↙ Bee houses can result in the proliferation of pests like pollen mites.

Bee Houses

Once reserved for only the most serious insect enthusiasts, bee houses designed for cavity-nesting bees have grown in popularity in recent years. Big box stores have marketed these mini bee hotels as solutions to pollinator decline. But are they helpful or hurtful? The short answer is it depends. Bee houses that can be deconstructed and properly sanitized each season can help to support cavity-nesting insects like mason and leafcutter bees. However, many commercially available bee houses are constructed with bamboo tubes glued securely in place, making it difficult (or downright impossible) to remove and sanitize the cavities. Diseases and pests like pollen mites can be passed from one generation—or one cavity—to the next when tubes are reused. Well-intentioned bee houses and insect hotels can also create a buffet for hungry

predators who won't need to travel far to find a feast among the many critters who will be nesting so closely together. It's best to support native bees by planting what they love and by stewarding your landscape to support bee and pollinator habitat. If you're keen to include a bee house in your wildlife garden, be sure to select one that allows for the removal and replacement or sanitation of cavities between nesting seasons.

Chapter 8

CREATE A BIRD-FRIENDLY BACKYARD

Birds play important roles in ecosystems around the world. For starters, we can thank our feathered friends for helping keep many insect populations in check. Birds consume somewhere around 400 to 500 million tons of insects each year, which helps gardeners and farmers by controlling pests like grasshoppers, crickets, caterpillars, beetles, and aphids. Similarly, birds of prey like owls, hawks, and eagles help to regulate populations of small animals like rodents and snakes. And Johnny Appleseed is no match for their incredible tree-planting abilities. Birds like blue jays disperse thousands of seeds each year as they collect, store, and sometimes forget to retrieve their winter acorn cache, leaving some nuts to sprout new oak trees.

Population Plummets

Rachel Carson's release of *Silent Spring* in 1962 ignited the modern environmental movement with her dire warning about the decline of birds due to pollution and pesticide use. But since Carson first sounded the alarm about the effects of chemicals in our landscape, bird populations

Chickadee

have continued to drop. North America has lost one in four birds since 1970, amounting to three billion fewer birds gracing our skies today. In Europe and Australia, the outlook is equally sobering. A 2021 report led by the Royal Society for the Protection of Birds found that Europe has lost around 600 million birds since 1980, and the Australian Threatened Bird Index found that threatened and near-threatened bird populations in Australia declined an average of 60 percent between 1985 and 2020. As with many environmental issues, the reasons for bird decline are complex and intertwined.

Habitat Destruction

Land use change throughout the last century has resulted in the loss of many natural areas. Forests, wetlands, and grasslands have been replaced with farms, cities, and suburbs, pushing wildlife to the margins of shrinking habitats. Birds rely on specific habitats for breeding, nesting, and foraging, and alteration and destruction of these habitats has serious consequences for their survival. Habitat destruction often leads to increased competition for limited resources, as birds are forced to compete with other species for food and shelter, and habitat fragmentation can lead to isolation and inbreeding, which reduce genetic diversity and further weaken bird populations.

Window and Building Strikes

Strikes occur when birds fly into human-made structures, like windows and buildings. According to the National Audubon Society, building collisions account for up to nine percent of bird deaths in North America annually, resulting in as many as one billion bird fatalities every year.

The conversion of natural habitat to farmland has negatively impacted wildlife by replacing the habitats they need to thrive.

....

OPPOSITE
Window strikes occur when birds, like this American goldfinch, fly into windows.

....

During the day, birds may mistake reflective surfaces for open sky or vegetation, flying into buildings where they are injured or killed. Species that eat insects are at increased risk of building strikes because they are attracted to flying insects that congregate around building lights.

Light Pollution

Of the 4000 species of birds that seasonally migrate, the majority fly at night. As the world becomes more developed with each passing year, nocturnal migrators are faced with increased light pollution. Defined as artificial light in the night sky, light pollution causes millions of bird fatalities every year by drawing birds into cities and suburbs where they are at increased risk of building strikes. This excess light can also disrupt biological clocks by mimicking daylight during the shorter days of winter, inviting birds to fly home too early in the season. When birds arrive early to their summer breeding grounds, it can create misalignment in food and resource availability as plants and insects may not yet be available for feeding.

THE LONG HAUL

Migratory birds, or those that travel from one habitat to another on a seasonal basis, account for around 40 percent of avian species. For some, this annual trip is short. The dusky grouse travels a mere 30 miles during its altitudinal migration from its winter home in mountainous pine forests to its summer home in bottomland deciduous woodlands. For others, migration is an extraordinary feat. Flying from the Arctic Circle to the Antarctic Circle and back again, the Arctic tern can travel more than 25,000 miles each year during migration.

Across North America, migratory songbirds take to the skies each fall to move south for the winter. In spring, these commuters return to their summer breeding grounds in the north. When conditions are ideal, avian migrations can grow so large and dense that Doppler radar is able to detect them. While Arctic terns and dusky grouse might not be visiting your backyard during their annual migrations, a diversity of songbirds is likely stopping by to rest and refuel during their arduous journeys north and south. By providing the resources these migrators need, you can help birds make the long haul between their summer and winter homes, ensuring their survival and successful reproduction.

Pest Control

Birds and other wildlife are often injured or killed in efforts to control undesirable pests in the home landscape. Widely used to control pests in agriculture, neonicotinoids pack a particularly bad punch for birds. The chemical, which is coated on crop seeds before planting, is taken up by the plant's vascular system and expressed in the plant's tissue, nectar, and pollen. When birds eat the seed, or feed on insects that visited treated plants, they are at risk of pesticide ingestion. Over time, this exposure to the chemical can lead to reproductive issues and may lead to impaired orientation, affecting the birds' ability to migrate. Pesticides can also harm birds by reducing the availability of prey like insects, rodents, and other small animals that they feed on. But chemicals aren't the only problem. Birds can also become entangled in pest control devices like glue traps, which are usually intended for rodents. Even when they are found quickly after entrapment, birds often suffer fatal injuries from these accidents.

Invasive Species

Non-native, invasive species disrupt entire ecosystems. Invasive plants, like multiflora rose and Japanese honeysuckle, create dense thickets in forests and grasslands that impede movement, replace shelter, and outcompete native plants that provide important food sources for birds.

Predation by cats is also of great concern, and the impacts of free-ranging felines is not confined to birds alone. Outdoor cats kill as many as four billion birds and 22 billion mammals annually (Loss et al., 2013). You might think that Fluffy would never kill, but even cats that are well fed have a predisposition to hunt and kill birds and other small wildlife including lizards, chipmunks, and mice.

Insect Declines

There is a common misconception that birds feed primarily on berries, nuts, and seeds. But 96 percent of terrestrial bird species feed their young insects. According to Doug Tallamy, professor of entomology and wildlife ecology at the University of Delaware, a single breeding pair of chickadees will feed their clutch between 6000 and 9000 insects (mostly caterpillars) in the two and half weeks it takes to raise their brood. Unfortunately, habitat destruction, pesticide use, urbanization, agricultural intensification, and light pollution are causing insect populations around the world to decline, compounding the impacts of these environmental issues for many birds.

Japanese honeysuckle creates dense thickets in the forest understory and replaces wildlife food and habitat. ↓

Insects such as this black swallowtail caterpillar make up the majority of a young bird's diet. ↘

Give Birds a Wing Up

Welcoming birds into your backyard has many benefits, including kickstarting a hobby for the entire family to enjoy—birdwatching. To create a backyard oasis for birds, it's essential to create the habitats they need to thrive while also minimizing threats that put them at risk for injury, illness, and death. Start by ensuring that birds have access to the basics—food, water, and shelter.

Food

Like all wildlife, birds need consistent access to high quality food sources. One of the best ways to provide a feast fit for birds is by planting native trees, shrubs, and flowers that will produce year-round access to berries, nuts, and seeds. And because native plants support more insects than non-native plants, you'll help ensure that birds have access to the food that they need to successfully rear their young by planting native. While you're working to restore native plants at home, consider hanging some bird feeders, which can be especially helpful

FROM TOP
Creating an oasis for birds at home can kindle a passion for birdwatching.

An American goldfinch enjoys eating anise hyssop seeds.

SKIP THE RED DYE

While the vibrant red color of commercial hummingbird nectar may appear attractive, these artificially dyed nectar solutions can have detrimental consequences for hummingbirds. Often found in store-bought nectar mixes, red dye can pose health risks to birds, including the potential to cause organ damage. Opt instead for hummingbird feeders made from colorful glass or plastic and prepare a homemade nectar solution by dissolving one part sugar with four parts boiling water. This solution closely resembles the natural sucrose content of floral nectar, creating a safe and nutritious food source for these small avian visitors. Ensure that the mixture has completely cooled before filling and hanging your feeder.

FROM TOP

Colorful hummingbird feeders are enough to attract these small birds.

Skip the red dye in hummingbird nectars and use a brightly colored feeder instead.

for birds that stick around throughout the cold winter months. Including a variety of birdseed mixes and types of feeders will ensure that you attract a diversity of birds.

Water

Birds use birdbaths and other water features, like small ponds, to drink and to clean debris from their feathers. While a simple dish or pedestal birdbath will attract birds to your yard, baths with aerators or small fountains will be more enticing as birds are naturally attracted to moving water. Moving water will also stay fresher for longer, reducing the need for daily cleaning and replenishment. For those with more space, creating a small wildlife pond in your garden also provides fresh water for birds. If you live in a region where winter brings freezing temperatures, installing a heated birdbath will ensure feathered friends have access to fresh water year-round. And placement of your birdbath matters, too. Place your water source in a shady spot to prevent water from overheating, because who wants to drink warm water on a hot summer day?

A birdbath or small wildlife pond with a stream or waterfall will attract birds with the sound of moving water.

Shelter

Native trees and shrubs provide natural shelter for birds to nest and rear their young. But nesting boxes can also provide wonderful shelters for a diversity of birds. Different bird species prefer different types of nesting boxes, so providing the right kind of shelter for the species you're hoping to attract is key. As colony nesting birds, for example, purple martins prefer large, multi-unit houses. Wrens, chickadees, and titmice, on the other hand, prefer smaller, simpler homes. Not sure what type of nesting box is best? Managed by the Cornell Lab of Ornithology, nestwatch.org provides an interactive tool that will help you uncover which species of birds you're likely to attract in your region and offers plans for building your own nesting boxes to attract them. They also offer resources for identifying bird species as well as information about managing predators and invasive species.

Prevent Window Strikes

Birds are more likely to collide with windows if they can't see them. You can make windows more visible by applying decals or other visual markers, such as hanging wind chimes or streamers in front of the windows on your home. You can also break up window reflections with screens, which will help to make windows more visible to birds. Spring and fall migration times pose the greatest risk for bird strikes, so take extra precautions to prevent birds from colliding with windows by turning off lights in homes and offices and closing your curtains and blinds overnight during these times of year.

Keep Cats Indoors

Keeping cats indoors might be a controversial topic for some. But the fact remains: cats kill wildlife. Keeping cats indoors eliminates the opportunities they have to hunt and kill wild prey, while also protecting your beloved pet from dangers like cars and predators. If your cat needs a bit of fresh air to stay happy, consider using a leash or harness for daily walks, or install a cat enclosure or "catio" in your yard.

FROM TOP
Many birds, like this house wren, will enjoy constructing their nest in a nesting box.

Installing window decals can break up window reflections and prevent bird strikes.

Keeping cats indoors prevents unnecessary predation on birds and other small wildlife.

A LITTLE HOUSEKEEPING GOES A LONG WAY FOR BIRDS

Washing the dishes and vacuuming the floors might not be your favorite way to spend time, but a little routine housecleaning goes a long way when creating a safe and livable space. Like us, birds have some creative ways of keeping their homes clean too. Rather than defecating in the nest, many baby birds produce a fecal sac—a literal bag of poop—that parents will collect in their beak and dispose of away from the nest. But while bird parents are keen to keep it clean, there are certain things they can't do, like scrub algae out of the birdbath or ensure last year's residents didn't leave anything behind when they vacated the nest. That's where you can help. These routine cleaning recommendations will keep birds happy and healthy.

BIRDBATHS Replace water every two to four days. Use a jet pressure hose to remove algae as needed and scrub with a natural cleaning solution once or twice per month or as needed. Keep it bird safe by cleaning with a mixture of nine parts water, one part vinegar or use a mild soap with water. Be sure to rinse thoroughly after cleaning.

BIRDFEEDERS Clean birdfeeders every two weeks. Tidy under your feeders by removing fallen seeds, hulls, and feces. For hummingbird feeders, replace the sugar solution every few days (or daily in high temperatures) to prevent the buildup of bacteria. Allow to fully dry before adding food.

NESTING BOXES Remove debris and nesting materials after birds have vacated the nest. For birds with multiple broods in a single season, it's best to clean houses between broods if possible.

If birdbaths are prone to filling with debris, like fallen leaves, replace water daily.

Chapter 9

RETHINK PEST CONTROL

Whether you're planting for pollinators or growing your own vegetables, managing pests in the landscape is an important part of gardening. But it's also essential to recognize that not all imperfections in your garden are cause for concern. Holey leaves provide a cozy nursery for baby leafcutter bees. The caterpillars you find chewing your vegetables provide critical nutrition to nesting birds and their offspring. And even those seemingly pesky mammals, like skunks and mice, are important parts of the larger ecosystem. Rather than reach for quick fixes, homegrown conservation gardeners are encouraged to embrace the trails and traces left behind by insects and other wildlife and consider control methods only when absolutely necessary.

The Problem with Pesticides

Homeowners use a staggering 80 million pounds of pesticides per year in an effort to maintain monocultures of turfgrass and ornamental plants. These lawn pesticides account for the majority of wildlife poisonings that are reported to the Environmental Protection Agency each year. Pesticides are chemicals designed to kill or repel insects, fungi, weeds, or other pests, and though these chemicals are intended to control

The holes in this redbud leaf were carved by a female leafcutter bee provisioning her nest.

BUG ZAPPERS

Zzzt! Zzzt! Zzzt! That zapping sound might be a welcome addition to your backyard barbecue. After all, each zap accounts for another pesky mosquito that won't be sucking your blood as you feast on those brats. Or does it? Bug zappers are certainly effective at killing insects. Unfortunately, they are indiscriminate killers that often target the wrong kind of bug.

Bug zappers work by emitting UV light, which is meant to attract flying insects to their death by means of electrocution. In tracking residential use of six bug zappers over a ten-week period, one University of Delaware study found that, of the 13,789 insects killed, only 31 were biting flies including mosquitos. Instead, the zappers killed a rich diversity of beneficial bugs including predators, pollinators, and parasitoids (Frick & Tallamy, 1996).

If you're looking to repel mosquitos from your next outdoor event, spatial repellents, which release chemical deterrents into the air, or fans can more effectively target and prevent mosquitos from getting too close without causing unintended and fatal consequences for beneficial insects.

pests they can sometimes harm non-target organisms, or plants or animals that are not the intended target of the pesticide. Pesticides harm animals through direct ingestion or absorption through their skin or breathing tubes, but they can also harm animals indirectly through the food chain. For instance, an owl may be poisoned by rodenticide when it unknowingly feeds on a rat that ingested the chemical. The effects of pesticide use can extend far beyond the backyard too.

What you apply to your yard doesn't always stay in your yard. Each time it rains, pesticides and fertilizers can get washed away from your garden and into neighboring streams, rivers, and lakes where they pollute drinking water and fuel the growth of harmful algal blooms. Harmful algal blooms block sunlight from reaching underwater plants, which can lead to oxygen depletion in the water and create "dead zones" where no aquatic life can survive. Some pesticides can also kill off the natural predators of algae, such as fish and other aquatic organisms, furthering the harmful growth of algae.

A Different Approach to Pest Control

Integrated pest management, or IPM for short, is a method of pest control that strives to reduce the use of pesticides. It involves practicing pest prevention strategies that blend cultural, biological, and mechanical practices, along with the judicious application of pesticides only when absolutely necessary. IPM takes a holistic approach to pest management, aiming to strike a balance between effective control and minimizing harm to the environment.

Cultural Pest Control

The practice of cultural pest control involves using various gardening practices that help to naturally prevent the establishment, survival, or reproduction of pests. Some examples of this include eliminating areas of standing water to prevent mosquitos from laying eggs, correctly siting and rotating crops to prevent the spread of diseases such as tomato blight, and disinfecting garden tools to avoid transferring unwanted diseases from one area to another.

Biological Pest Control

Biological pest control involves using other organisms to help manage pest problems. Predatory insects such as lady beetles and lacewing larvae can help keep aphids, mealybugs, spider mites, and other pests in check, while parasitoid insects like wasps can help prevent caterpillars from feasting on your vegetables. By creating a welcoming environment for beneficial insects, you can create natural checks and balances in your home landscape that will promote ecological harmony and minimize your reliance on chemical control.

Mechanical Pest Control

Mechanical pest control refers to the use of physical means to manage unwanted pests. A hardy spray of water from the hose, for instance, can effectively dislodge pests from plants, while manually plucking Japanese beetles from plants can prevent them from ravaging your favorite flowers. For areas of the garden that are particularly sensitive, exclusion fences can prevent insects and other wildlife from accessing your plants.

Chemical Pest Control

There are times when pesticides might be warranted, but they should generally be used as a last resort and only when you're certain that you have a pest problem that requires the use of chemical control. If you decide that chemicals are necessary, choose products that are least toxic to non-target species and always follow label instructions carefully. It's best to apply chemicals during the cooler parts of the day like morning and evening, when fewer insects are out foraging and when risk of volatilization is minimized.

↑ Small insects, like this red-banded leafhopper, can be easily dislodged from plants with a spray from the hose.

← Robber flies, also called assassin flies, are incredible predators, feeding on a variety of garden pests, including leafhoppers, grasshoppers, and beetles.

Japanese beetle traps lure males by emitting a floral scent or a pheromone that mimics the scent of female beetles. While the traps will almost certainly capture copious numbers of the pest, they actually draw more beetles to your garden than would naturally occur, ultimately leading to increased plant damage. To manage Japanese beetles more effectively, it's better to focus on mechanical or manual control methods, like knocking beetles into a jar of soapy water. Putting a few drops of soap in the water will help break the surface tension and allow the beetles to sink, effectively drowning them.

Japanese beetle pheromone trap (left) and a Japanese beetle (right)

Getting Started with IPM

Practicing integrated pest management requires intimately learning about your garden. When you understand the life cycles of various insects and the threshold for feeding that your plants can tolerate, you'll be better prepared to identify and address emerging issues. For instance, if you're nurturing a balanced ecosystem, waiting a few days before hosing down plants at the first sign of aphids might reveal that lady beetles and other predatory insects will soon take care of the problem for you. Make a point to scout for pests each time you visit your garden and consider keeping a journal of your observations. This written record can help you to identify temporary or isolated issues as opposed to ongoing problems that might warrant control. It will also help in predicting when issues might arise, as you can track how pest populations fluctuate based on conditions like rainfall, temperature, or time of year.

If you observe an emerging issue in your landscape, take time to uncover the root cause so you avoid chasing symptoms of a larger problem. Consult with local experts if you need help identifying or confirming the presence of a pest. Online communities like iNaturalist and BugGuide are great resources that connect you to experts who can accurately identify pests and diseases. Your local extension office may also be able to offer recommendations for pest control and prevention.

Beneficial Predatory Insects

Beneficial predatory insects play an essential role in the garden ecosystem by providing natural pest control. Ambush bugs are adept hunters that patiently lie in wait on flowers for unsuspecting prey. Mantidflies are generalist predators that feed on a variety of small arthropods like spiders, making them efficient biological control agents. And lady beetles, with their voracious appetites for aphids, are effective in keeping pest populations in check, which minimizes the need for chemical pesticides in your wildlife garden. These beneficial predators, among many others, work together to maintain a balanced ecosystem. As you create an oasis for wildlife, be on the lookout for these beneficial insects.

Resembling a small praying mantis, mantidflies feed on a variety of arthropods in the garden, including spiders and mites.

As their name suggests, ambush bugs are ambush predators that lie in wait on flowers, attacking prey when they stop by for a sip of nectar.

Parasitoid wasps lay their eggs inside the eggs of other insects, like these brown marmorated stinkbug eggs, which wasp larvae will consume before they have a chance to emerge.

Lady beetles are voracious predators of insects like aphids, a common plant pest.

Spiders, like this peppered jumping spider, feed on a diversity of small insects in the garden.

Lacewing larvae strategically position themselves near clusters of aphids before consuming them.

Long-legged flies are stealthy garden predators, catching small prey, like thrips, whiteflies, and spider mites.

Dragonflies are one of nature's most efficient hunters, boasting a 95 percent catch rate.

MAIL-ORDER PREDATORS

Over the years, mail-order biological insect control has been touted as a great solution for managing garden pests like aphids, whiteflies, mealybugs, spider mites, thrips, and more. Mail-order insects often include predatory species like lady beetles, praying mantids, and green lacewing larvae. While these insects are known for their beneficial role in controlling garden pests, purchasing insects for release in the garden is not always the best option. In many cases, these commercially available species are not native to the area of release and will actually create more problems than they solve by outcompeting native wildlife for resources. And newly released insects are likely to quickly disperse before helping control any pests in your garden. Instead of purchasing beneficial insects online, create a welcoming environment for native beneficial insects to naturally establish.

Touted as biological pest control, Chinese praying mantises are indiscriminate predators that outcompete native species for resources in the United States, where they are non-native.

Give Your Garden a Fighting Chance

Attracting wildlife to the home garden might seem downright foolish. After all, deer, rabbits, groundhogs, and other hungry critters can quickly ravage the fruits of your labor. But gardening for wildlife and growing your own food at home need not be mutually exclusive endeavors. If you're keen to keep wildlife out of certain areas of your yard, there are ethical and sustainable ways to ensure Bambi doesn't make a meal out of your garden.

Managing Mammals

Whether they're used to protect a pollinator patch or a food garden, exclusion fences and barriers are one of the best ways to keep animals from munching prized plants. A tall fence can deter deer, while a shorter fence with smaller gaps may be suitable for protecting plants from rabbits and groundhogs. If you decide that a fence is your best option for protecting your garden, here are some considerations to ensure that the barrier is effective and long-lasting.

Height Determine the height of the fence based on the type of wildlife you are trying to exclude. If you're trying to keep out deer, the fence should be at least 8 feet tall. For smaller animals like rabbits or groundhogs, a fence 2 to 3 feet tall may be sufficient.

Material Choose a durable and strong material that can withstand the weather and animal pressure. Some common materials for wildlife exclusion fences include metal mesh or chicken wire, though you may opt for repurposed materials like old pallets.

Depth Make sure the fence extends deep enough into the ground to prevent animals from burrowing underneath it. Burying fencing to a depth of 1 to 2 feet is recommended.

Maintenance Consider the maintenance required for the fence to ensure its longevity. For example, metal fences may need occasional rust treatment, while wooden fences may need to be painted or stained every few years.

Cost Determine your budget for the fence and choose materials that fit within your budget. Low-budget fences may be friendlier to the pocketbook initially, but they may also need to be replaced more frequently.

Local regulations Check your local city ordinances to determine if there are any applicable regulations or permits required for building a fence on your property.

Utilities Call your national "Call Before You Dig" hotline to ensure that your utility lines, like gas and power, are visibly marked. This is vital to ensuring the safety of your project.

Avoid Traps

Traps may seem like a simple and effective solution to manage unwanted wildlife visitors, but they can be quite harmful, not to mention unethical. Many traps are designed to injure or kill animals. Sadly, they often end up harming non-target species. Even live traps turn deadly when animals are not freed quickly enough. What's more, trapping and relocating wildlife is not lawful in many areas. Instead of relying on traps, there are a number of alternative strategies for dealing with unwanted wildlife in the garden, including fencing, scent and noise

FROM TOP

If your gardening goals include growing your own food, building an exclusion fence to deter wildlife, like deer and groundhogs, can help ensure that you'll enjoy the harvest before it's eaten.

Using decoys in the garden can be an effective way to deter small mammals, like chipmunks and mice. Just be sure to move the decoy frequently so wildlife stay vigilant.

THE STICKY TRUTH ABOUT GLUE TRAPS

Glue traps work by using a sticky adhesive to immobilize any animal unlucky enough to make a wrong step. While they may seem like a quick and effective solution to a pest problem, glue traps cause immense suffering to animals, often resulting in a slow and painful death from starvation, dehydration, or exhaustion. In addition to their cruelty, glue traps often harm non-target animals, such as birds and insects, that may accidentally get stuck. Before reaching for a glue trap as a quick fix, consider alternative methods such as exclusion techniques that are safer and more ethical for wildlife.

deterrents, and making changes to your yard that will make it less attractive to the animals you want to discourage.

Install Tree Tubes or Barriers around New Plants

It can be difficult to establish shrubs and tree seedlings in the wildlife garden, especially if you have voracious deer in the neighborhood. Installing tree tubes or barriers around new plants can help by protecting woody species from deer browsing and antler rubbing. Tree tubes, also called tree shelters, act as physical barriers, making it harder for animals to access the tree's bark or leaves. This can be especially important for young trees, which are more vulnerable to damage and may not survive if they're constantly being browsed. For shrubs,

Tree tubes can prevent damage from wildlife, including deer and beavers.

larger mesh or wire barriers may be needed to keep wildlife from accessing branches.

Watch Your Waste

Trash can be a major source of attraction for wildlife, particularly raccoons. These beloved bandits are known for their fondness for rummaging through trash cans, leaving a mess in their wake. Unfortunately, they aren't the only wildlife attracted to waste. Squirrels, bears, coyotes, and even cats and dogs may be interested in tasting your trash. To prevent this, make sure the lid of your trash can is tight-fitting and can't be easily pried open. If needed, use bungee cords or other fasteners to ensure that the lid stays closed. If your trash can doesn't have a lid or the lid is broken, consider getting a new one or repairing the old one. Be sure to store your trash cans in a secure location like a garage or shed. If you don't have a garage or shed, put your trash cans in an enclosed area, such as a fenced-in backyard. This will make it more difficult for wildlife to access.

Since many animals are attracted to the smell of food, be sure to rinse out food containers before tossing or recycling them. A sprinkle of baking soda in the bottom of your trash can will help to neutralize odors and further deter wildlife from exploring your refuse. If you have a food garden or fruit trees, dispose of fallen fruit swiftly. Make sure compost bins are properly sealed and located away from the garden to avoid attracting wild animals. While it may be tempting to leave out food scraps or pet food to attract cute critters to your yard, remember it's best to create a thriving ecosystem so wildlife have access to what they naturally eat.

MOTH BALLS

People have been using moth balls for over a century to protect clothing from fabric-munching moths. Moth balls are typically made from either naphthalene or paradichlorobenzene, which are both toxic fumigants that volatilize at room temperature. They are designed to be used in airtight containers like garment bags, chests, or trunks to prevent vapors from spilling out into occupied rooms. Unfortunately, in an attempt to ward off undesirable critters, like snakes, some gardeners have resorted to using moth balls in home landscapes.

Using moth balls to repel wildlife from outdoor spaces like the garden is not only illegal, but unethical too. Not only can moth balls contaminate soil and water, they can also injure pets and wildlife when ingested. If you're up against a pest problem, it's best to find an appropriate solution like an exclusion fence to keep animals from digging, rooting, or eating sensitive plants or vegetables.

While some may find snakes a scary addition to the garden, their presence in your yard can be a sign of a healthy ecosystem.

Chapter 10

FLIP THE SWITCH ON LIGHT POLLUTION

Before electricity, people relied on fire as a source of light at night. But Benjamin Franklin's experiments with electricity in the 18th century illuminated the way for the invention of electric lights in the early 1800s. By 1879, Thomas Edison's patent of the incandescent light bulb allowed electric lighting to become a viable option for homes and businesses around the world. And the invention of the incandescent bulb was just the beginning. In the years that followed, new lighting technologies were developed, paving the way for the world to grow a bit brighter with each passing decade. Unfortunately, this artificial light has disrupted the delicate balance of nature and wildlife.

The Problem with Too Much Light

Light pollution occurs when there is too much artificial light in the night sky. There are three main types of light pollution that affect our night skies. Glare is a type of pollution that occurs when lights produce excess brightness, which causes visual discomfort. For people, glare from unshielded light can present safety issues as it reduces the ability to see clearly at night. Sky-glow is the buildup of light that shines up into the atmosphere. This form of light pollution

is most apparent in urban areas where dense populations of people live and work. Light trespass occurs when light shines outside of the intended area that it's meant to brighten. If you've ever experienced the garish glow of a streetlight or neighbor's security light shining brightly into your window at night, then you've been a victim of light trespass.

Though the phenomenon is not new, the effects of light pollution have grown as urbanization has become more widespread and intense. Between 2011 and 2022, global sky brightness grew by nearly ten percent per year (Kyba et al., 2023). More than 80 percent of the world's population now lives under light-polluted skies, and that figure jumps to 99 percent in the United States and Europe. Streetlights, building lights, and advertisement lights, like those found on billboards, glow brightly in the night sky, and in many cases it's not merely the presence of light at night but the misdirection of light that causes concerns. When light fixtures are not properly aimed or shielded, they can shine light upwards into the sky rather than where they are meant to illuminate.

The Dark Side of Light

While lighting technology has provided an important creature comfort for people around the globe, it has also created unintended consequences for both people and wildlife. Too much artificial light at night disrupts the natural circadian rhythms of humans, leading to sleep disorders, increased stress levels, and a decrease in overall health and well-being. It's also a major contributor to wasted energy. DarkSky International estimates that at least 30 percent of all outdoor lighting in the United States is wasted, amounting to $3.3 billion in wasted energy costs and the release of 21 million tons of carbon dioxide into the atmosphere each year. This not only has negative environmental impacts, but also contributes to higher energy bills for individuals and businesses. While people can often escape the impacts of light pollution, wildlife are not so lucky. Darkness is critical for nesting, reproduction, and migration in many species.

Moths

Most moths are nocturnal, relying on the cover of darkness for essential activities like foraging, mating, and navigation. The pervasive glow from streetlights, buildings, and other human-made sources interferes with moths' ability to orient themselves, as they often use the moon and celestial cues for navigation, causing them to circle artificial lights, which not only wastes their energy but also increases their vulnerability to predation by other nocturnal creatures like bats. Additionally, the exposure to constant light disrupts the moths' circadian rhythms, affecting feeding and reproduction. Disrupted mating behavior can lead to a decline in moth populations that creates a cascade of effects on the ecosystems they inhabit.

Ever wonder why moths tend to congregate around your porch light? Some entomologists believe that moths use transverse orientation, or the practice of keeping a fixed angle on a distant source of light, to orient themselves in the night sky. In a naturally dark sky, moths orient using the moon. But in light-polluted

A SPARK OF HOPE

DarkSky International is a non-profit organization that was founded in 1988 with the goal of preserving and protecting the night skies for present and future generations. The organization works to reduce the impact of light pollution on the environment and human health by promoting responsible outdoor lighting practices, educating the public about the impacts of light pollution, and advocating for policies that reduce the phenomenon. They also designate areas as "International Dark Sky Places," which are locations that have made a commitment to preserving and protecting their night skies. These areas serve as a model for other communities and help raise awareness of the importance of reducing light pollution.

Unshielded lights can attract nocturnal insects, such as moths, disrupting their natural feeding and mating behaviors.

skies, they can use streetlamps or porch lights to navigate. Keeping a fixed angle on the moon is easy for moths due to its far-off distance in the night sky. But keeping a fixed angle in relation to something like a street lamp, which is considerably closer than the moon, requires moths to constantly shift their angle to maintain their relative position to the source of light, causing erratic flight patterns and wasting their energy.

Birds

Every year, millions of birds fall victim to light pollution. Excess light at night leads to disorientation, collisions, and even death for many species. For nighttime migrators, light pollution can lead birds to fly in circles and expend valuable energy that should be reserved for their long journeys. Brightly lit buildings can also attract birds, resulting in window strikes. During periods of heavy migration, a single building can kill hundreds of birds per week. Light pollution can also interfere with the synchronization of bird migration patterns by mimicking longer periods of daylight and disrupting their biological clocks. This causes some birds to migrate too early and arrive at their breeding grounds at the wrong time of year, which can negatively impact their chances of reproduction and survival.

Amphibians

Exposure to artificial light at night reduces hatching success in tadpoles and increases their susceptibility to parasites. Light pollution can also lead to quieter nights by reducing the call frequency of some species of frogs, impacting their ability to find a mate and reproduce. The

Fireflies

Habitat fragmentation and destruction have played key roles in firefly decline, but light pollution is also a leading cause of the loss of these glowing insects. Fireflies use biolumi-nescence to communicate and attract mates. Each species of firefly has its own unique light pattern that serves as a sort of firefly Morse code, signaling their identity and availability to potential mates. When the sun goes down, male fireflies flash courtship signals into the night sky, while females lie in wait amongst tall grasses or other vegetation. When a female firefly is interested in a potential mate, she'll send a reciprocal flash, drawing the male to her location. Light-polluted environments may make it difficult for fireflies to attract a mate, as excess lights cause confusion and difficulty finding flashes.

↖ Some frog species, like green frogs, have been shown to reduce calling behavior in light-polluted environments.

↓ Fireflies need darkness to find mates.

outlook for salamanders and toads is equally dim. Light pollution causes some salamanders to spend their nights hiding in leaf litter rather than foraging for food, while the excess night light causes juvenile American toads to stay active throughout the night when they would normally rest, leading to wasted energy and stunted growth.

Trees

Trees and plants rely on a regular cycle of light and dark to regulate their growth, flowering, and seed production. Light pollution can interfere with these processes, leading to changes in the timing of plant growth and behavior. Exposure to artificial light can cause trees to flower earlier in the spring, increasing their risk of blooming before the threat of frost has passed. This can lead to reduced seed production and lower sur-vival rates. In temperate regions, trees growing directly under street lamps have even been shown to retain their leaves longer as the arti-ficial light mimics longer periods of daylight.

A CLOSER LOOK

From their intricate wing patterns that are designed for camouflage in moonlit landscapes to their keenly developed antennae, which allow them to find a mate from miles away, moths exhibit a remarkable diversity in size, shape, and color. While some species live up to their reputation for being dull and drab, others, like the giant silk moths of North America, wear flamboyant colors that make them some of the most beautifully charismatic creatures you might be lucky enough to spot in the wildlife garden.

As caterpillars, giant silk moths are voracious eaters, feeding on the foliage of their host plants, which usually includes trees like oaks, hickories, maples, walnuts, willows, sycamores, sassafrases, and persimmons. Adults do not have mouths and therefore do not feed. They have just one purpose in life—to reproduce. Light-polluted environments threaten moths by drawing them to lights, where they become easy targets for predation by birds and bats. Removing sources of light pollution and planting native host plants in your garden can create safe spaces for these colorful insects to thrive.

BELOW
Io moth

OPPOSITE, FROM TOP
Luna moth

Regal moth

Rosy Maple moth

FROM TOP

Light pollution can disorient aquatic insects, like
mayflies, causing them to
lay their eggs on surfaces
like asphalt instead of in
bodies of water.

⋯⋯⋯⋯⋯⋯⋯⋯⋯⋯⋯

Sea turtle hatchlings are
attracted to light sources,
causing them to head away
from the ocean.

⋯⋯⋯⋯⋯⋯⋯⋯⋯⋯⋯

Aquatic Insects

Many insects, including mayflies, damselflies, dragonflies, caddisflies, and stoneflies, spend their immature life stages in the water. In their larval form, these aquatic insects remain attached to stream substrate during the day to avoid being eaten by predators like fish and birds. Under the darkness of night, they float downstream with the current in a practice known as drifting. Drifting provides a safe way for aquatic insects to move safely from one location to another, since fish cannot see the insects floating above them in the darkness.

When light pollution illuminates the surface of the water from above, however, it silhouettes the insects as they move, making it easier for fish to find and eat them. Light pollution can also confuse aquatic insects, luring them to lay eggs on reflective surfaces like asphalt instead of in bodies of water like lakes and streams.

Sea Turtle Hatchlings

Coastal cities are popular getaway spots for vacationers. But as beaches around the world have grown brighter, the risk for sea turtles has grown. Sea turtles rely on natural light cues to navigate and complete their life cycle. Artificial lights on the beach can disorient sea-turtle hatchlings, causing them to move away from the ocean and toward danger. Adult sea turtles are also at risk, as light pollution interferes with their ability to make their way back to the ocean after nesting, increasing mortality.

Lights Out

Before you let light pollution dim your outlook on creating a nature-friendly yard, here are a few ways to curb excess light at home. Start by flipping the switch. Turning off unnecessary outdoor lights at night can help restore darkness to the skies. It also saves electricity, which can mitigate the impacts of climate change. Turn porch and flood lights off entirely when not needed, and if it doesn't pose unnecessary risk, consider using a motion detection setting on your security lights so that they only turn on when motion is detected. And don't forget about garden lighting. Those fanciful fairy lights might provide a bit of whimsy in the garden, but be sure to turn them off when the garden party is over.

Light polluted sky - - - - - - - - - - - - - - - - - → Visible night sky

Unacceptable
Unshielded

Very bad

Bad

Better

Best
Fully shielded + timer
or motion sensor

← For lights that must remain on overnight, use shields to ensure that light is directed downward.

↙ If it's safe to do so, switch security lights to a motion detection setting so they turn on only when needed.

← ↑ Swapping cool-toned outdoor lights for warmer bulbs can be an inexpensive and effective way to curb light pollution at home.

For lights that must stay on overnight, install appropriate shields and covers so that light is directed downward toward its targeted area rather than up into the sky. Swapping cooler-toned bulbs for warmer ones is also a good idea. Lights in warmer tones such as amber, yellow, and red have a lower color temperature and are more effective at reducing light pollution compared to traditional white or blue-toned lights. These warmer toned lights are also less attractive to insects like moths and provide better nighttime visibility by reducing glare.

Outdoor lights can be problematic for wildlife. But if you're not careful, indoor lights can lead to light pollution too. If you're a night owl and enjoy late nights, be sure to draw the curtains or close the blinds so indoor light doesn't become outdoor light.

Chapter 11

POWER DOWN

From electric-powered lawn care tools to outdoor lighting and décor, the management and maintenance of outdoor spaces often comes with a host of energy-zapping practices. But you might be surprised to learn that on average, more than half of your home's energy usage goes toward indoor heating and cooling. When thoughtfully designed, your yard can play a role in reducing your overall energy footprint, which can cut carbon emissions and mitigate the impacts of climate change for people and wildlife.

Keep Your Cool

Strategically selecting and placing trees, shrubs, and other vegetation around your home can create a microclimate that will help to reduce your reliance on the electrical grid, not to mention cut down on heating and cooling costs. Trees are natural shade providers, blocking direct sunlight from reaching your home during hot summer months. And natural windbreaks can help reduce the force of cold winds during winter and minimize heat loss from your home when it's cold.

Plant for Shade
Large deciduous trees such as oaks, maples, and birches offer an excellent solution to your landscape by providing ample shade during the hot summer months while allowing sunlight to filter through during the cooler seasons

Large shade trees, like these pin oaks, provide morning shade for this east-facing home. ↑

Strategically placed trees can reduce your reliance on heating and cooling naturally. →

after their leaves have fallen. Positioning these trees on the east and west sides of your home can effectively block the intense morning and afternoon sun, reducing the heat gain in your indoor spaces and lowering your reliance on air conditioning. Shadier landscapes also promote water conservation, as the moisture retained by shaded soil is less prone to evaporation. The cooling effect of shade extends beyond your property, too, influencing the surrounding environment and potentially reducing the urban heat island effect in your community.

Create Windbreaks

Windbreaks are carefully planned rows of trees, shrubs, or other vegetation planted to shield your property from strong winds. By creating a barrier against prevailing winds, windbreaks can effectively mitigate the force of cold air, reducing heat loss and enhancing the energy efficiency of your home. In fact, according to the United States Department of Energy, strategically placed windbreaks can reduce winter heating costs by up to 30 percent. And the benefits don't stop there. Windbreaks can safeguard your home against wind damage caused by storms, reduce soil erosion, and provide habitat and food for wildlife. And for those who enjoy solitude and privacy, they can also reduce noise and screen your property from nosy neighbors.

Evergreen trees and shrubs such as spruces, pines, and junipers are popular choices for windbreaks because they offer year-round protection thanks to their dense foliage. However, deciduous trees that shed their leaves in the winter will allow sunlight to penetrate during colder months, helping warm your home naturally. As with all planting, consider the mature height and spread

TREE CARE

When planting for shade and windbreaks, consider the long-term growth of the species you choose. Be sure to provide adequate space for plant growth and check your trees regularly to prune any weak, dead, or diseased branches that could pose a risk during storms. As climate change brings more frequent and severe storms to our doorsteps, maintaining tree health is increasingly important. Well-maintained trees with strong, healthy branches are better equipped to withstand the forces of wind, rain, snow, and ice, preventing storm damage and ensuring the safety of your home and community. Routine tree care will also help sustain the shade canopy and prolong the benefits that your trees provide.

of your chosen plants to ensure that they will offer desired protection. Proper spacing between plants is also essential to avoid competition for sunlight, water, and nutrients, but you'll want to space plants close enough to avoid gaps where wind can cut through.

Choose Energy-Efficient Lawncare Equipment

From mowing and blowing to trimming and tilling, maintaining turfgrass lawns comes with a price. And with more than 40 million acres of lawn to manage in the Unites States alone, it's no wonder why. According to the Environmental Protection Agency, Americans use around 800 million gallons of gas—and spill an additional 17 million gallons—in our efforts to maintain turfgrass lawns each year.

HEAT ISLAND EFFECT

Trees and vegetation provide natural cooling through shading and transpiration. In cities, where trees have been largely replaced by impervious surfaces like asphalt, concrete, and metal, heat is absorbed and retained, leading to increased temperatures compared to surrounding rural areas. This phenomenon is known as the heat island effect, and it has a variety of consequences ranging from adverse impacts on public health (as higher temperatures increase the risk of heat-related illnesses) to heightened energy consumption driven by the escalating demand for cooling in urban environments. Cities prone to the heat island effect often experience rolling blackouts or brownouts, which are arranged power outages or reductions in power, as utility companies are forced to balance the power supply. These power outages further exacerbate concerns for public health, particularly for vulnerable populations like older adults and low-income communities who might not have resources to handle the heat.

Planting trees and creating green spaces in urban areas can provide shade, reduce surface temperatures, and enhance air quality, all while restoring important habitat for wildlife. Implementing cool roof technologies, such as the use of reflective materials or green roofs, can further minimize heat absorption by buildings, cooling the surrounding environment and lessening the impact of the heat island effect.

Urban and suburban neighborhoods designed with street trees can drastically reduce heating and cooling needs while providing wildlife habitat.

Thankfully, there are alternatives to using gas-guzzling machines to upkeep your yard.

Go Electric

Swapping gas-powered lawn care equipment for electric tools can significantly reduce the carbon footprint associated with maintaining your home landscape. Electric lawn mowers, trimmers, and leaf blowers offer a cleaner and more sustainable alternative to their gas-powered counterparts by producing zero direct emissions and eliminating the release of harmful pollutants into the air. Not only do electric tools help improve air quality, but they're usually much quieter too, creating more peaceful communities by reducing noise pollution. While there is an initial investment in switching to electric tools, the long-term benefits outweigh the costs by mitigating climate change and improving the overall health of neighborhoods.

Go Manual

If you're looking to kick carbon to the curb for good, consider putting a little elbow grease into your lawncare routine. Electric tools offer a great alternative to gas-powered ones, but unless you're powering your home through renewable energy like wind or solar, even electric tools are powered by electricity generated through carbon-intensive means, like burning coal. Opting for manual lawn care equipment can help to avoid this carbon conundrum. Manual equipment includes tools like reel mowers, hand shears, manual edgers, and rakes. These tools not only eliminate the need for fossil fuel consumption, but also operate near silently, eliminating noisy equipment.

FROM TOP
Replacing a gas leaf blower with an electric one can help curb carbon emissions.

Electric leaf blowers can be corded, like this one, or battery operated, which provides more flexibility in movement around the yard.

Reel mowers might seem like a tool of the past, but people are switching to these manual tools as a means of cutting out carbon-intensive landscaping practices.

Chapter 12

GET WATER-WISE

Throughout history, the availability of water has played an important role in the development and survival of communities. The first civilizations emerged and settled near major rivers, recognizing the vital role that access to water played in food production as well as social and economic development. But as civilizations advanced and modern plumbing systems emerged, our use of water transformed. The ability to transport water across vast distances allowed people to overcome geographical limitations and expand settlements into areas previously deemed uninhabitable. Sadly, this convenience has led to a sense of complacency around water usage—and water wastage.

Water is naturally replenished through the hydrological cycle, but demand for water has increased exponentially with population growth and industrialization. As a result, careless water consumption practices have strained water supplies and damaged ecosystems. The average American family uses 320 gallons of water every day, with around 30 percent of this water being devoted to outdoor uses like landscape irrigation. What's worse, about 50 percent of the water we use outdoors is wasted due to inefficient watering methods and leaky faucets.

Landscape irrigation accounts for 30 percent of water usage in the United States.

With deep root systems that effectively anchor the soil, native plants act as natural sponges, increasing the soil's capacity to absorb water and mitigate runoff. When it rains, water filters slowly through the soil instead of quickly running off impervious surfaces, like concrete or compacted lawns. Landscapes anchored by native plants are better equipped to handle heavy rainfall and minimize the risk of flooding, all while reducing your reliance on routine watering. That said, it's important to note that newly installed native plant gardens will still need to be watered regularly until fully established.

FROM TOP
Wildlife, like this great blue heron, depend on healthy aquatic habitats.

Pollutants, like pesticides and fertilizers, can travel from your home landscape to rivers, lakes, and wetlands by way of small streams.

Going with the Flow

A watershed is an area of land that drains water from rainfall and snowmelt into small waterways, including creeks, streams, and tributaries. These small waterways eventually make their way to larger bodies of water like lakes and rivers, and those lakes and rivers provide drinking water to local communities while furnishing critical wildlife habitat for countless species. Pre-development, much of the water that flowed through watershed from rainfall or snowmelt would be soaked into the ground where it would be naturally filtered. But as forests and wetlands have been converted into subdivisions and developments, pervious surfaces have been replaced with impervious ones, like rooftops, driveways, and roads. This means that water has fewer places to soak into the ground, leading to runoff, which occurs when there is more water than the land can absorb. According to the United States Environmental Protection Agency, runoff is one of the greatest threats to clean water in the nation because it pollutes our waterways by carrying fertilizers, pesticides, oils, sediment, and bacteria to streams, rivers, lakes, and oceans before it can be treated.

Water-Wise Strategies

Fresh water is a finite resource. As the global population grows, the demand for water will only continue to rise, underscoring the importance of adopting water-wise landscaping practices. Water-wise gardening is not just a buzzword, it's a fundamental shift in how to approach home gardening. By selecting the right plants for your landscape and adopting water-conserving techniques such as drip irrigation, mulching, and rainwater harvesting, you can create beautiful and bountiful gardens that require significantly less water than traditional gardening methods, safeguarding water resources for future generations while protecting wildlife that depend on freshwater habitats. Here are a few ways to make your landscape water-wise.

Plant a Rain Garden

Rain gardens are shallow, sunken garden beds that capture water from impervious surfaces, like your home's roof, and absorb it into the ground. These gardens are planted with a variety of deep-rooted native grasses, flowers, and shrubs that can reduce runoff by temporarily holding rainwater and allowing it to soak into the ground slowly, reducing the risk of flooding and erosion, and filtering pollutants and sediment before they reach natural waterways. Rain gardens also provide food and habitat for wildlife including birds, butterflies, and beneficial insects.

Rain gardens are strategically designed with berms, or raised edges, that hold water and allow it to slowly filter into the ground.

FIX YOUR FAUCETS

At first drip, it may seem like a minor issue, but a leaky faucet can waste thousands of gallons of water each year. Stop the leak by conducting a visual inspection of your outdoor faucets and hoses regularly. Pay special attention to the connections between the hose and the faucet, as well as any other attachments, scouting for visible signs of leaks such as dripping or pooling water. Sometimes, fixing a leak is as simple as tightening things up a bit.

Before winter arrives, disconnect and drain your hoses to prevent damage caused by freezing and thawing. When temperatures warm in the spring, reconnect the hoses and inspect for any newly emerged issues. Fully extend the hose and turn on the water. Look for signs of water seepage or spraying from holes or cracks that may have developed over the colder months. Small holes can be patched with special hose-repair tape or repaired by cutting the damaged portion of the hose out and joining the two sections of hose with a coupling.

Small holes in hoses can be easily repaired without the need to purchase a new hose.

The size and shape of your rain garden will depend on the size of your yard, the amount of rainfall you typically receive, and the total drainage area that you'll be filtering water from. A good rule of thumb is to create a rain garden that is approximately ten percent of the size of the drainage area that feeds it, with a depth of around 6 inches, but there are a host of factors to consider when planning your garden. When designed right, a rain garden should drain water within twelve to 48 hours, preventing issues that may arise with standing water, like breeding mosquitos. For detailed instructions on how to design and install a rain garden suited to your yard, visit your local soil and water conservation district or county extension office.

Improve Irrigation

Swapping garden sprinklers for a drip irrigation system is an easy way to conserve water in the wildlife garden. Unlike sprinklers that spray water indiscriminately, drip irrigation delivers water directly to the root zones of plants, minimizing water loss through evaporation and runoff. This targeted approach ensures that water is used efficiently and effectively by eliminating water wastage on non-target areas, such as foliage

Newly installed native plant gardens will need to be watered regularly until they are fully established.

or sidewalks. Timing is also of the essence. By watering in the early morning or evening hours, when temperatures are typically lower and the sun is not at its peak, you'll minimize water loss by reducing the risk of evaporation before water reaches the roots of your plants where it's needed most.

Measure Rainfall and Soil Moisture

You could use the time-honored tradition of sticking a finger into your garden's soil to determine when it's time to water, but tools like a rain gauge and soil moisture monitor can provide a more accurate reading of your garden's irrigation needs. A rain gauge collects and measures rainfall and offers an important clue to how much water your garden has received in a given period of time. But rainfall is only one piece of the puzzle, especially considering that different soil types retain moisture differently. Dense clay soils retain water longer than sandy or loamy soils, so understanding how long your soil stays wet will also be helpful in determining when your plants might need an extra drink.

Even if you aren't certain of your soil's makeup, you can use a soil moisture meter to determine your soil's moisture content at a given moment. A soil moisture meter uses a long probe to measure electrical conductivity of the soil. Because water conducts electricity well, a higher electrical current means more moisture in the soil, whereas a lower current provides a clue to dryer soils. Understanding how much rain your garden has received and the moisture levels of your soil will help you to avoid the common pitfalls of over- or under-watering. Of course, understanding the moisture needs of

your plants will also provide an important clue to how often you should be watering.

Group Plants with Similar Water Needs

Different plants have different watering needs, which means that you might need to skip an overly prescriptive watering routine to ensure that all your plants get exactly what they need. One way to approach this is by creating zones based on the unique water requirements of your plants. This will allow you to tailor your watering practices to meet the specific needs of each zone.

FROM TOP

Soil moisture meter
....

Rain gauge
....

RAIN CHAINS

Unlike a traditional downspout, rain chains are designed with a series of small cups, links, or funnels that channel water from the roof of a building to the ground in a decorative way. These downspout alternatives originated in Japan, where they were called *kusari doi* and were traditionally made of bronze. Today, rain chains come in a host of materials, from copper and stainless steel to aluminum and even glass, and can be designed to fit a wide range of personal tastes. Rain chains not only look beautiful, they also serve a functional purpose of slowing the flow of rainwater before it reaches the ground, reducing soil erosion. And by pairing the chain with a rainwater harvest basin, you can collect water to be later used for nourishing plants or replenishing ponds or birdbaths.

When grouping plants with similar water needs, consider factors such as soil type, sun exposure, and climate conditions. Drought-tolerant plants that thrive in sandy soil and full sun, for example, can be grouped together in a south-facing garden bed that receives direct sunlight and has well-draining soil. On the other hand, moisture-loving plants that prefer shady areas and moisture-retentive soil can be grouped separately in a different zone. Grouping plants with similar water needs simplifies your watering routine and allows you to focus your attention and resources on the specific zones that require water at a particular frequency. This targeted approach saves time, reduces water usage, and ensures that each plant receives the appropriate amount of moisture for optimal growth. Ultimately, it all boils down to planting the right plant in the right place.

Install a Rain Barrel

A rain barrel is a container that collects rainwater from your rooftop and stores it for later use in your landscape. From large plastic drums to more subtle containers that resemble wood barrels or terra cotta pots, rain barrels come in a variety of shapes and sizes. Choose one that meets your water needs and aligns with your personal garden aesthetic. Before installing the barrel, ensure the ground is level and sturdy enough to support its weight when full. It might be a good idea to elevate the barrel with sturdy bricks or cinder blocks for easier access to the spigot. Next, install a diverter on your downspout to redirect rainwater into the barrel. Get creative with where you install your barrel. While positioning a rain barrel at a downspout is quite

common, you can also harvest condensation from your air conditioner. Once it's in place, be sure your barrel is securely positioned to prevent it from tipping over.

Mind Your Mulch

Mulching your garden beds is an easy way to reduce water usage by creating a barrier between the soil and the sun, which helps retain soil moisture by slowing down evaporation and keeping the soil cool. This means that plants are able to access water—and the nutrients within—for a longer period, thereby reducing the need for frequent watering. Mulch offers a multitude of other garden benefits too, like suppressing weeds and adding organic matter back into the soil as

it decomposes. This organic matter improves the soil's structure, which in turn allows water to soak into the ground more easily. It also provides a food source for beneficial microbes in the soil, which aid in nutrient uptake by plants. Each year, add two to three inches of mulch to your garden beds to maximize its benefits and account for decomposition.

Not all gardens need mulch. In fact, if you're mimicking nature by planting a prairie or meadow garden, your plants will likely be dense enough that they'll act as a sort of living mulch, suppressing weeds and creating a soil moisture barrier without any additional amendments. If you do decide to mulch your garden, always opt for natural, non-dyed and chemical-free mulch, and avoid the use of inorganic materials like rubber or plastic, which will not break down naturally.

↖ Harvesting water from air conditioner condensation is a creative way to get water-wise.

← This rain barrel harvests rainwater from a downspout.

Chapter 13

DON'T IGNORE YOUR DÉCOR

Whether it's putting up a holiday tree or carving a creepy jack-o-lantern, decorating for the holidays is a time-honored tradition that brings us joy. For some, decorating for the holidays is a simple way to have fun, spread cheer, and lift spirits. For others, it's a way to honor ancestors and pass down cultural practices from one generation to the next. But while our holiday decorations might spread cheer and joy to us, they sometimes have unintended consequences for wildlife.

The Downside of Decorations

Holiday decorations generate an immense amount of waste. Many decorations, like outdoor lights, ornaments, plastic pumpkins, and giant yard inflatables, are made from non-biodegradable materials that can take hundreds of years to break down in a landfill. What's worse, much of what we use to decorate our homes for the holidays is only used for a short time before being tossed in the trash. In fact, estimates suggest that Americans produce 25 percent more waste between Thanksgiving and New Year's than during other times of the year. Add in the packaging for all those decorations and it's easy to see how wasteful holidays can become. Then there are the carbon costs.

The transportation of decorations from factories to stores and eventually to your home contributes to climate change through carbon

emissions, adding to their environmental footprint. Decorations like inflatable yard ornaments and elaborate light displays also require electricity to operate. While the energy consumption of individual decorations may be small, the collective energy usage of holiday adornments across the globe can be significant.

Reducing the environmental footprint of your holiday celebrations can be an easy way to make your landscape more climate- and wildlife-friendly. This can include choosing decorations made from sustainable and biodegradable materials, using LED lights, and opting for reusable decorations instead of disposable ones. It also means finding creative ways to repurpose single-use decorations so they don't end up rotting in the landfill. By making more sustainable choices during the holidays, you can continue spreading cheer all year long while also taking care of the planet.

Being mindful of your holiday decor can help curb carbon and protect wildlife.

Sleigh Your Winter Holiday Impact

For many people around the world, the winter season is one of the most joyous times of the year, but it can also be one of the most unsustainable. From energy-sucking holiday lights that set our homes aglow on chilly winter nights to the abundance of plastic packaging that protects the cherished gifts under our trees, the holiday season can take a toll on the environment. Here are some ideas that can help you lessen the impact of your holiday festivities.

Embrace Energy-Efficient Décor

Your holiday light display might not consume enough electricity to cause a citywide power outage (we're looking at you, Clark Griswold), but that doesn't mean you can't take steps to reduce your power consumption while getting into the holiday spirit. The two most common types of holiday light bulbs are LED and incandescent. LED lights, which use light-emitting diodes, consume around 75 percent less energy

MIRRORING NATURE

Many of our holiday decorations are designed to mimic nature, which is a bit ironic considering we often opt for artificial versions of these nature-based adornments. For Christmas, we trim our homes with plastic Christmas trees and greenery. For Halloween, we entangle polyester spider webs through our trees and shrubs. For the Fourth of July, we blast fireworks into the sky amidst fields of flashing fireflies. When it comes to nature-inspired holiday décor, the dupes aren't always worth it, especially when they could harm wildlife. Fortunately, there are easy ways to reduce your impact and swap the fabricated finery for the real deal.

than incandescent bulbs, which use filaments that produce heat. Because most of the energy incandescent bulbs produce goes toward heat production rather than light, they are far less energy efficient. These inefficient bulbs can also grow hot enough to pose burn and fire

LED lights (left) are more energy efficient than incandescent bulbs (right).

THE LEGEND OF THE CHRISTMAS SPIDER

The legend of the Christmas spider is a Ukrainian folktale that has been adapted and passed down through generations across eastern Europe and beyond. The legend tells the story of a poor, widowed woman and her children during the great famine in Ukraine who had no decorations or gifts to put under their Christmas tree. One night, a spider descended from the ceiling and spun glittering web over the branches of their tree. When the woman and her children awoke the next morning, they were amazed to discover that the spider had adorned their tree with beautiful web. When the other villagers saw the tree, believing it to be a miracle, they too began decorating their own trees with spider webs. From then on, it became a Christmas tradition to decorate trees with webs and spiders as a symbol of hope and the miraculous power of faith. For those who opt for a real holiday tree, you might be lucky enough to find a real spider that will adorn your branches with glittering web.

A small jumping spider sits atop the star on a real Christmas tree.

risks, especially when in direct contact with flammable materials (you know, like a dead tree). LED lights generally do not produce heat, so they remain a safer option, especially when trimming a real tree. What's more, LED lights can last up to 25 times longer than their incandescent counterparts, reducing the amount of waste that gets sent to the landfill each year.

Choose a Nature-Friendly Christmas Tree

In the United States alone, around ten million artificial trees are purchased each year. Sadly, after only a few years of use, many of these fake trees end up in a landfill as non-biodegradable trash. Artificial trees may be convenient, but the fake foliage can't hold a candle to the benefits that real trees provide to wildlife. Unlike their artificial counterparts, real trees are a renewable resource, providing habitat for wildlife while supporting a diverse ecosystem of plants and animals while they grow. If the Lorax on your shoulder has you screaming, "But I speak for the trees!", consider that on many tree farms, when one tree is cut, a new one (sometimes even two or three) is planted in its place. As they grow, these trees absorb carbon dioxide and other pollutants from the air, which can help improve air quality. Real trees that are locally grown and harvested drastically reduce greenhouse gas emissions associated with the transportation of these decorations from one side of the globe to another. And a real tree can continue to spread joy long after the holiday season.

It might be tempting to toss your tree to the curb alongside the ribbons, wrapping paper, and cardboard boxes from Christmas morning, but your tree can provide valuable shelter and nesting materials for birds and small animals over the winter. If you already have a brush pile tucked away in an inconspicuous spot in your yard, you can simply add your holiday tree to the pile (after removing lights and ornaments, of course). Alternatively, many cities and towns offer programs that collect and recycle real trees. Through these programs, trees are chipped or composted and will enjoy a second life as mulch or soil, hopefully in a native plant garden.

Real trees can be added to a brush pile to create wildlife habitat.

PLANT YOUR CHRISTMAS TREE

If you love the idea of decorating with a real tree but aren't keen to compost it or add it to the brush pile after the holiday season is over, why not buy a tree that can be planted in your wildlife garden instead? Unlike stem-cut trees, dug trees whose roots have been balled and burlap-wrapped can be planted outside after the holiday season. In just a few years, you'll enjoy your own mini evergreen forest that provides shelter and food for various wildlife, from birds seeking refuge in branches to insects like fireflies that thrive in the darkness of the coniferous understory.

Just be sure you're accounting for the extra size and weight when selecting your tree. With the added weight from soil and roots, dug trees can weigh up to several hundred pounds and will need to be displayed in a large watertight container. And if you're accustomed to decorating for Christmas as soon as Thanksgiving is over, think again. Dug trees will only last indoors for about seven to ten days, so you'll want to hold off on decking the halls until closer to the holidays. When you're ready to plant, place the tree in an unheated garage or shed for a few days so it can acclimate back to cooler temperatures, which is especially important for those in colder climates.

Make the Fall Holidays More Sustainable

Halloween is the one time of year when you can get away with erecting an enormous skeleton in your front yard without side eyes from the neighbors. Or perhaps you enjoy a more subtle display of impeccably carved jack-o'-lanterns on the porch. Whatever your preference, Halloween décor can generate unnecessary waste and create unintended—even deadly—consequences for wildlife. Being more mindful of how you celebrate the spooky season will ensure that wildlife can visit your yard safely while you get your trick-or-treat on.

Leave Webs to the Real Spiders

Despite their numerous benefits, spiders are often regarded as one of the scariest animals on the planet, so it's no surprise that these eight-legged arthropods have inspired an array of Halloween décor. After all, as much as 15 percent of the world's population suffers from arachnophobia, or fear of spiders. Each October, fake spiders and polyester spider webs adorn homes in an effort to spook trick-or-treaters. But fake spider webs can be a literal death trap for small birds and other wildlife, with the potential to cause injury or death should they become entangled in them. It's best to leave the webbing to the real spiders.

Wildlife can become entangled in fake spider webs, leading to injuries or worse.

Other decorations, especially when not disposed of properly, can wind up in natural areas and waterways. If you do decide to decorate your home for Halloween, be sure to dispose of all items responsibly and purchase decorations that can be reused again and again. For items that can't be reused, recycle what you can and dispose of non-recyclable materials in a garbage bin. Be sure to cut items into small pieces to prevent wildlife entanglement and avoid placing materials in areas where they may be accessible to wildlife.

Don't Pitch Your Pumpkins

From Halloween jack-o'-lanterns to Thanksgiving pies, pumpkins are a beloved symbol of the fall season. When trick-or-treating is over and the fall feast comes to an end, what becomes of all those pumpkins that were precisely picked just a few weeks earlier? Before you pitch those gourds, consider giving them a second chance. More than one billion pounds of pumpkin waste ends up in landfills every year, but you can keep your spent pumpkins out of the landfill by composting them instead. Pumpkins are high in nitrogen and other minerals that can help enrich the soil. By composting these fruits, you can create a natural fertilizer that supports your garden. Cut or smash your pumpkins into smaller pieces and remove the seeds (if you're worried about sprouting your

SAVOR THE SEASON

After carving jack-o'-lanterns, you might be tempted to toss all the ooey innards of your pumpkins in the compost bin. But there's a tasty treat lurking within. Before composting your pumpkin guts, scoop out the seeds and rinse them thoroughly under cold water to remove any clinging pumpkin flesh. Allow the cleaned seeds to dry overnight or pat them dry with a clean kitchen towel. Toss the seeds with a bit of olive oil or melted butter and season them with your choice of flavors. Try salt for a traditional approach or spice things up with a mixture of garlic powder, paprika, and your favorite hot sauce. For a sweet twist, try seasoning with a bit of sugar and cinnamon. Spread the seasoned seeds in a single layer on a baking sheet and roast them for 20 to 30 minutes in a preheated oven at 300°F (150°C), stirring occasionally to ensure even roasting. Enjoy your batch of crispy, golden-brown pumpkin seeds as a healthy, homemade snack or sprinkle them on soups or salads for a bit of crunch.

own pumpkin patch) before throwing them in the compost pile.

If you're not up for composting your gourds, toss them in the garden instead. Many animals enjoy eating pumpkins and will happily feed on the flesh and seeds. You can also hollow out the pumpkin and fill it with birdseed to create a natural birdfeeder. Just be sure to avoid using pumpkins that have been painted or treated with toxic materials, like bleach, to make them last longer.

↖ A variety of wildlife, including squirrels, raccoons, deer, and opossums, will feed on cut-up pumpkins in the garden.

Make a birdfeeder out of a pumpkin by cutting the gourd in half, scooping out the seeds, and filling with birdseed. →

Choose Fireflies over Fireworks

With each passing year, more conservationists, wildlife rehabbers, and pet owners call for bans on fireworks, and with good reason. Firework shows may only last for a few fleeting moments, but the big booms and flashy lights of these Fourth of July light shows can have devastating and long-lasting effects on wildlife. Not only do fireworks emit metallic compounds into the air, they also create litter and waste that ends up in natural areas and waterways. The earsplitting explosions can also cause stress, anxiety, fear, and disorientation in wildlife. In an attempt to escape from the ruckus, some animals flee their nests, leaving behind offspring. Others become lost and wander into roadways where they risk injury or death. Unfortunately, wildlife are not the only ones negatively impacted by fireworks. Loud booms and flashes of light can trigger stress, anxiety, and fear in our pet dogs and cats too. The displays can be equally troubling for people who have sensory-processing disorders, respiratory conditions, and those who suffer from post-traumatic stress disorder. What's worse, when poorly planned, fireworks have the potential to ignite devastating wildfires, adding to the long list of reasons to skip the flashy festivities.

If you're looking to make your next Fourth of July celebration more wildlife-friendly, pack up the barbecue and head to the nearest forest or field to watch a magical display of nature's own fireworks—fireflies. Fireflies, also known as lightning bugs, are neither flies nor true bugs, but rather a type of beetle known for its ability to produce light. They live in tropical and temperate regions of every continent except Antarctica. In the United States, fireflies thrive in warm, humid environments like wooded areas, marshes, and fields near ponds, rivers, and streams. While all species of fireflies glow as larvae, only the adults of some species emit light. This process of producing light is called bioluminescence and serves different functions depending on the insect's life stage. In larvae, bioluminescence is believed to ward off predators by offering a clue to fireflies' toxicity. In firefly adults, flashing is usually a method of attracting a mate.

While fireflies occur in all lower-48 states in the United States, many of the western species are diurnal, which means they are active during the day and may communicate with pheromones rather than flashing lights. The best time to look for flashing fireflies is at dusk and into the late evening during the summer months when they are most active. You may even be able to find them in your own backyard if you're stewarding your landscape for wildlife, or you can visit a local park or nature preserve to see them.

Chapter 14

CULTIVATE YOUR DINNER PLATE

Agriculture is the foundation of human civilization and has undeniably played an important role in nourishing and sustaining societies throughout history. But the rapid intensification of modern agriculture has also created significant environmental challenges. The quest to feed a growing global population has led to widespread adoption of industrial farming practices, which prioritize high yields and efficiency, sometimes at the expense of the environment.

Large-scale monoculture farming has led to soil erosion and degradation. Extensive irrigation has resulted in the over-extraction of groundwater. Fertilizer runoff into rivers and lakes has caused harmful algal blooms and "dead zones" where aquatic organisms cannot survive. And the conversion of forests, grasslands, and wetlands into farmland has resulted in the destruction of valuable ecosystems and the loss of countless plant and animal species. What's more, the average distance food travels before reaching our dinner plates is astounding, with processed food traveling over 1300 miles and

fresh produce traveling more than 1500 miles before consumption. While the globalization and centralization of food production has offered consumers a wider diversity of foods available at the grocery store, the long-distance journey between where food is grown and where it's consumed has also resulted in increased carbon emissions.

Growing some of your own food at home or in a community garden plot can reduce the impact of food production. While you may not be able to grow all of your meals at home, growing some of your own produce can help offset

Whether grown in pots, raised beds, or in the ground, food gardens can be adapted to fit your unique space. ↑

Growing your own food is a reliable way to enjoy your favorite produce all season long. →

environmental costs of conventional food production while giving you more control over what you're growing. You'll also be able to experiment with new produce varieties while reducing the cost of groceries during the growing season.

Planning Your Vegetable Garden

Before heading outside to sow seeds in the ground, think about your gardening goals and create a plan. By planning your garden strategically, you can maximize space, optimize crop yields, and cultivate a diverse array of vegetables and herbs that will keep your family satisfied all year long. Selecting the right location for your food garden is the most important first step toward a bountiful and successful harvest. Here are a few things to consider when selecting the perfect spot to plant produce:

Sunlight Exposure Select a location that receives at least six to eight hours of direct sunlight per day. Most vegetables and herbs thrive in full sun, so choose a location that won't be shaded by towering trees or buildings for long periods of the day.

Soil Quality Assess the soil's texture and drainage. Look for loamy soil, which is a balanced mix of sand, silt, and clay. Avoid areas with compacted or waterlogged soil, as it may hinder root development of your crops. If needed, conduct a soil test to better understand the makeup and health of your soil.

Proximity to Water Choose a spot close to a water source for convenient irrigation.

SHOP LOCALLY

For foods you simply can't grow at home, consider shopping locally at a farmers market or participating in a community supported agriculture (CSA) or crop-sharing program. Farmers markets bring together a variety of local food producers for easy access to local shopping, while CSAs allow community members to pledge financial support to a local farmer in exchange for a share of the harvest. If you don't have the space to grow your own food garden, these can be great alternatives to reducing the carbon footprint of what you eat.

Wind Protection Consider nearby structures or natural barriers that offer protection from strong winds. Wind can damage plants and dry out the soil quickly, so a sheltered location, like next to a fence, might be beneficial, so long as it doesn't block sunlight.

Accessibility Ensure that the chosen spot is easily accessible for activities like planting, weeding, and harvesting. Plan the layout carefully, leaving

RAISED BED GARDENING

Whether you're a seasoned gardener or a beginner, raised bed gardening offers a practical approach to growing a variety of vegetables, herbs, and flowers. Raised bed gardening involves planting in elevated garden beds rather than directly in the ground. Beds are typically constructed from wood, cement blocks, or metal and form a contained and defined growing area. Planting in raised beds offers many benefits, including improved soil drainage, better control over soil quality, and reduced weed growth. The elevated height also makes gardening more accessible, especially for gardeners with physical limitations. When combined with other space-saving

techniques like square-foot gardening, raised beds can help to maximize planting efficiency and allow for easy organization of different crops.

Gardening in raised beds allows for control of soil while increasing accessibility for those with limited mobility.

enough room between rows for easy movement and future expansion if desired.

Existing Vegetation Avoid areas with large trees or dense shrubs that can shade out your plants. If you're growing in the ground as opposed to raised beds, competing root systems might hinder growth of your crops.

Legal Restrictions Check local regulations and homeowners association guidelines to ensure that vegetable gardening is permitted and compliant with any community restrictions.

Creating Healthy Soil

Whether you're planting in the ground or in raised beds, creating and maintaining healthy soil is the cornerstone of a successful vegetable garden. Soil provides an essential foundation for robust plant growth, nutrient-rich produce, and overall garden health. It also acts as a carbon sink, sequestering carbon dioxide from the atmosphere, which helps mitigate climate change. Moreover, healthy soils are better at retaining water, reducing runoff and erosion, and filtering pollutants than poor soils.

Building healthy soil begins with incorporating organic matter, such as compost or well-rotted manure, which will enrich the soil's fertility and structure. These organic materials nourish the soil's microorganisms, encouraging their growth and activity. As these microorganisms break down organic matter, they release vital nutrients in forms that plants can readily use. In turn, plants exude sugars and other substances through their roots, feeding the soil microbes and establishing a harmonious exchange.

Reducing the use of synthetic fertilizers and pesticides is another important part of maintaining a thriving soil ecosystem for your garden. While these chemicals may offer quick fixes, they can disrupt the natural balance of soil life by harming beneficial microorganisms and causing long-term damage to the soil structure. Instead, choose organic gardening practices like composting or mulching with leaves or natural wood chips and using natural pest control methods.

Choose Your Crops

When selecting crops, consider your local climate, growing season, and the specific conditions of your garden space. Some vegetables, like peas and spinach, thrive in cooler temperatures, while others, like tomatoes and peppers, can take the heat of summer's sun. Take note of the average temperatures and frost dates in your region to help guide you in choosing what crops to grow and when to plant them safely outdoors. Also be sure to evaluate the amount of sunlight your garden receives throughout the day. Different vegetables have varying light requirements, with some favoring full sun exposure and others tolerating partial shade.

Be sure to also consider the size and layout of your garden space. While crops like sprawling squash or vining tomatoes require ample room to spread, others, such as compact lettuces or herbs, can be tucked into smaller garden beds or containers. Planning your garden layout with consideration for each crop's spacing needs ensures that plants have enough room to grow without competing for resources. Most important, select crops that are staples in your household or ones that you and your family are

HEIRLOOMS

Growing heirloom vegetables is akin to cultivating a piece of living history in your garden. Heirloom vegetables are prized for their unique flavors, diverse appearances, and historical significance. These varieties have been passed down through generations, often for a century or more, maintaining their original traits and characteristics. Unlike modern hybrid plants, which are usually bred for uniformity and shelf life, heirlooms offer a rich tapestry of tastes, colors, and textures. Whether it's the vibrant hues of a Cherokee Purple tomato or the delicate sweetness of a Moon and Stars watermelon, heirlooms offer a unique and rewarding experience that allows you to savor the flavors of the past and preserve a legacy of biodiversity and cultural heritage for the future.

are already established, giving you a head start in the growing process. This method is particularly beneficial for plants that have a longer time to maturity, like peppers and tomatoes. The downside, however, is that the selection of plant varieties may be more limited when choosing transplants, and it may be harder to find specific heirloom or unique varieties.

Vegetables and herbs that are easy to start from seeds include carrots, beans, lettuce, radishes, and cucumbers. These plants tend to germinate quickly and grow well when sown directly in the garden soil. Crops that benefit from transplanting include squash, tomatoes, peppers, eggplants, and certain herbs like basil and parsley. These plants require a longer growing season and are best started indoors to give them a head start and ensure they have enough

excited to try. Growing crops that you enjoy eating will undoubtedly heighten your gardening experience and encourage you to savor the fruits of your labor.

Next, you'll need to decide whether to grow crops from seeds or transplants. Starting vegetables from seeds provides a wider range of plant varieties and allows you to control the entire growth process, from germination to harvest. Seeds are often more affordable than buying transplants, but starting from seed requires more time, care, and attention, as seedlings need proper conditions and maintenance until they are strong enough to transplant outside in the garden. On the other hand, using transplants can be a convenient and time-saving approach, especially for gardeners with limited space or a shorter growing season. Transplants

time to mature and produce a bountiful harvest. Whatever you choose to grow, be sure to research each crop and decide which method of planting makes the most sense for you.

Maximize Your Growing Space

Gardening in a small space? Maximize your planting room through space-saving techniques like square-foot gardening or vertical gardening. Square-foot gardening involves dividing the garden into manageable square-foot sections, each dedicated to a specific crop. By carefully planning the arrangement of crops and efficiently utilizing space, square-foot gardening allows you to grow a diverse range of vegetables in a compact area. This method minimizes wasted space and optimizes productivity, as every inch of the garden is purposefully planted. Square-foot gardening can also reduce pressure from weeds and pests since the tight planting arrangement eliminates open soil areas that could otherwise attract unwanted intruders.

Vertical gardening provides similar advantages by capitalizing on vertical spaces in the garden, allowing crops to grow upwards. By utilizing vertical structures such as fences,

↖ Growing vining crops like cucumbers up a trellis can save space in smaller vegetable gardens.
· ·

← Square-foot gardening is a great way to maximize growing space.
· ·

COMPANION PLANTING

Companion planting is a time-honored gardening practice that harnesses the relationships between different plant species, capitalizing on their ability to provide support for one another. The technique involves strategically planting compatible plants alongside each other, which can promote natural pest control, improved pollination, enhanced nutrient uptake, and structural support.

Aromatic herbs like basil, thyme, and rosemary can be powerful repellents for unwanted garden pests such as aphids, mosquitoes, and carrot flies when planted near susceptible crops like tomatoes and carrots. Marigolds, with their pungent odor, act as natural pest deterrents that can drive nematodes and whiteflies away from the herb garden. Flowers like sunflowers and zinnias attract pollinators, such as bees and butterflies, which facilitates the cross-pollination of nearby crops and boosts fruit production. Legumes such as peas and beans have a remarkable ability to fix nitrogen from the air into the soil through their roots, and when interplanted with nitrogen-hungry crops, like leafy greens or brassicas, contribute essential nutrients to the surrounding plants and reduce the need for synthetic fertilizers. And taller plants like corn can provide much-needed support for vining plants like pole beans. Ultimately, companion planting allows you to create a balanced garden where your plants can help each other thrive.

Planting flowers like marigolds can deter pests away from valuable crops.

walls, or sturdy stakes, you can cultivate vining vegetables like cucumbers, beans, or peas, along with tall plants such as tomatoes. This approach is particularly useful for small urban gardens, balconies, or patios, where horizontal space is limited.

enjoy a continuous supply of fresh vegetables and herbs, prolonging the growing season and making the most of your region's growing conditions. It is especially beneficial for fast-growing vegetables, like lettuce and radishes, that can be harvested and replanted quickly.

Maximize Your Yield with Succession Planting

Succession planting is the art of carefully timing and coordinating multiple plantings to ensure a continuous harvest throughout your growing season. Rather than planting everything at once, succession planting involves staggering plantings at regular intervals. As one crop is harvested, the space is quickly filled with something new. Succession planting allows you to

↖ Fast-growing crops like lettuces can be harvested and replanted multiple times throughout the growing season.

← Creating a garden plan with approximate harvest and planting times can ensure that your garden produces all season long.

Harvesting and Preserving Your Yield

Harvesting, enjoying, and preserving the yields from your garden is arguably the best part of growing your own food. Make a point to visit your garden daily and check for crops as they reach peak ripeness. You'll want to harvest produce at the right time to ensure the best flavor, nutritional content, and overall quality. Timing is key, as waiting too long to harvest could result in overripe, bitter, or spoiled crops. If you have a small garden, you might be consuming fresh produce as quickly as it's harvested. But larger gardens might produce more than you can eat at one time, allowing you to experiment with ways to preserve your harvest.

Canning is a popular method for preserving fruits and vegetables, allowing them to be stored in sealed jars for long periods without refrigeration. Pickling, which is a form of canning, involves immersing vegetables in a vinegar-based brine, adding a nice tanginess to produce like cucumbers, carrots, radishes, and onions. Freezing is an excellent option for preserving vegetables like cauliflower, peas, asparagus, corn, and green beans. By blanching your vegetables before freezing, you can retain their colors, textures, and nutritional content until ready to eat. Drying or dehydrating fruits and herbs is another traditional food preservation technique that removes moisture, preventing spoilage and resulting in long-lasting and concentrated flavors. Whatever food preservation method you choose, be sure to follow recipes and instructions to avoid spoilage and foodborne illness.

Pickling can help preserve vegetables like cucumbers and radishes. ↑

Canning is a great way to preserve fruits like raspberries, blueberries, and grapes. →

OPPOSITE
Drying and preserving herbs allows you to enjoy the tastes of the garden all year.

Chapter 15

SAVE YOUR SEEDS

Saving seeds can help save the planet. Okay, that might seem a bit hyperbolic, but saving seeds from your garden to plant next year can help preserve genetic diversity, build species resilience in the face of a warming climate, and reduce waste from commercially packaged seeds. Seed saving offers financial advantages, too. Rather than buying new seeds each season, you can plant your next garden with seeds you've saved, which translates to long-term cost savings. Ultimately, seed saving epitomizes the ethos of a sustainable garden by fostering a holistic and self-sufficient approach to growing food for both you and wildlife. If that sounds enticing, here are some ways to get started.

Saving Seeds from the Food Garden

Over the last century, as industrial agriculture has replaced small family farms and backyard gardens, hybrid seeds have become the new norm. In an endeavor to produce genetically uniform and high-yielding crops, many traditional and genetically diverse plant varieties

have become endangered or lost. Today, just twelve plants supply 75 percent of the world's food, and more than 90 percent of crop varieties—and the diversity of form and flavor they brought to our food—have disappeared. You can help reverse this trend by saving seeds from the heirloom and open-pollinated crops you grow, which can also help maintain genetic diversity within plant populations, ensuring their resilience against pests, diseases, and climate change.

Saving Vegetable Seeds

Vegetable seeds are collected either wet or dry. To save wet seeds, like those from tomatoes or peppers, leave fruit on the plant until fully ripe or overripe. After harvesting, cut open the fruit and scoop out the seeds. Depending on the crop type, you'll need to rinse seeds in water or ferment them in a jar with water for a few days. Fermentation can help break down the gel-like substance that encases seeds from fruits like tomatoes. This process also helps separate the seeds from the pulp. After rinsing or fermenting, allow seeds to dry for several weeks on a hard surface like a plate. Avoid using paper towels, as seeds can stick to the fibers and become difficult to remove. Once dry, store seeds in an airtight container and keep in a cool, dry place until you're ready to plant.

Dry seeds are a bit simpler to collect and save than wet seeds. Dry seeds, like those from peas and beans, are found in pods or husks that can be left to naturally dry in the garden. To harvest dry seeds, wait until the pods turn brown and brittle, but be sure to harvest before

HYBRIDS VS. HEIRLOOMS

Hybrid plants (sometimes denoted as F1 hybrids) are the result of crossbreeding between different varieties or species. Hybrids are usually bred for specific traits such as color, size, or disease resistance. Seeds collected from hybrids will not reliably produce plants with the same characteristics as the parent plant. Instead, they may exhibit a wide range of characteristics, meaning you'll be in for a surprise each time you grow plants from saved hybrid seeds. It's also important to note that some plants are patented and therefore protected as intellectual property of the creator. Collecting and propagating seeds from patented plants is illegal without express permission from the patent holder. For this reason, it's best to focus on saving seeds from open-pollinated or heirloom varieties, which have been cultivated over generations. Unlike hybrids, open-pollinated and heirloom varieties maintain their genetic stability over time, ensuring that the plants you grow from these seeds will be identical to their parent plants as long as they don't cross-pollinate with other varieties of the same species.

While some plants are self-pollinated, others require cross-pollination via insects, wind, or water to reproduce. Saving seeds from self-pollinated crops like peppers, tomatoes, beans, and peas is a great place to start for beginner seed savers. These crops have perfect flowers, meaning each flower contains both male and female reproductive parts. However, it's

good to note that self-pollinating varieties may still cross-pollinate when other varieties of the same crop are planted nearby. For example, pollen from a banana pepper can successfully pollinate a bell pepper and result in the development of a lovely fruit. But growing seeds from this fruit will result in peppers with both bell and banana pepper traits (which may or may not be what you're after). If you want more of the same delicious bell peppers, you'll need to ensure that you space different crop varieties far enough apart to avoid cross-pollination.

If you're planning to plant multiple varieties of the same open-pollinated crop in your vegetable garden, it's important to space varieties far enough apart to avoid cross-pollination if you intend to save seeds.

FROM TOP

To save seeds from peppers, leave fruit on the plant until fully ripe or overripe.

Fermenting tomato seeds for a few days helps break down the gel-like substance that encases the seeds.

Legume pods can be left on the plant to dry before collecting seeds.

Once dry, break open the seed pods and allow to fully dry before storing.

pods crack open and drop seeds. It's best to harvest after a few days of rain-free weather so pods are dry. After harvesting, gently break open the pods to release the seeds. Allow the seeds to continue drying in a well-ventilated area for several weeks before storing.

Saving Herb Seeds

While you might be tempted to pinch off flower heads as soon as you see them so that your herbs continue to produce all season long, let a few plants go to flower if you plan to collect seeds to use next growing season. Keep an eye out for your biggest and healthiest plants and allow their flowers to set seed. Generally, flowers should be left to dry and turn brown before harvesting, but plants that readily self-sow—like chives, oregano, cilantro, and basil—may need to have seed heads collected early to avoid seed drop (unless you'd prefer to let nature take its course). Check on plants daily so you know when they're ready. When the time comes to harvest, carefully snip the entire flower head and place it in a paper bag. Allow the flower heads to continue drying in the bag for a few weeks until the seeds can be easily shaken out and stored.

CLOCKWISE FROM TOP

Chive flower

. . . .

Dried chive flower head

. . . .

Harvested chive seeds

. . . .

Saving Seeds from the Pollinator Garden

Collecting seeds from your vegetable and herb gardens is an inexpensive and easy way to feed your family for years to come. But why stop there? Collecting and planting seed from your pollinator garden can feed your wild neighbors. Native plants grown from seed collected from local wild-type plants will be better adapted to your specific climate and soil conditions. Over time, the seeds you save and grow from one year to the next will gradually become acclimated to your garden's unique microenvironment, resulting in plants that are more robust and fruitful. As a bonus, this process fosters a reciprocal relationship between you and your garden, as the plants you cultivate evolve to thrive in the conditions you provide, and you learn to adapt your practices based on their needs.

When native plants start to produce seeds, it's time to begin the collection process. Avoid collecting too early or too late by carefully monitoring your plants and observing when the seed pods or heads begin to dry and turn brown. This indicates that the seeds are mature and ready for harvesting. If seeds are left too long, there's a good chance birds will get to them before you do. To collect the seeds, gently cut or shake the seed pods or flower heads over a clean, dry container to release the seeds. Some plants may require a little more effort, such as gently rubbing between your hands to release the seeds. For prickly seed heads, wear work gloves to avoid painful pricks. After collecting the seeds, remove any debris or chaff by using fine mesh screens or strainers. Allow the seeds to completely dry before storing in a cool, dry place.

When it comes time to plant the seeds you've collected, be sure to research the unique needs of each species. While some seeds may benefit from scarification (breaking the outer coating), others may need to be stratified (exposed to cold temperatures to stimulate germination). Follow guidelines for each plant species to ensure successful germination and growth.

Purple coneflower ↑

....

Dried purple coneflower flower head. To save its seeds, snip the dried flower and gently rub it between your fingers to release the seeds. →

....

COLLECTING MILKWEED SEEDS

Timing is everything when it comes to collecting milkweed seeds. Summer's blooms usually give way to seed pods in the late summer or early fall. You'll want to wait until pods have begun to split open, revealing seeds nestled within silky, parachute-like fibers, but before the wind has had a chance to carry seeds away. Patience is key, as waiting for the right moment guarantees higher seed viability.

FROM TOP
Seeds of common milkweed grow in large bulbous pods on the plant. • Ripe milkweed seeds • Unripe swamp milkweed seeds.

SEED SWAPS

Need help sourcing local seeds? Or perhaps you've collected a lot of your own seeds and would like to share the wealth with your community. Participate in a seed swap! Seed swaps are fun ways for gardeners to exchange the seeds they've saved from their own gardens with others looking to do the same. The practice of sharing seeds not only promotes the diversity of plants you're growing in the garden, but it can also help you connect and share resources with other local gardeners. Find seed swap events by reaching out to local garden clubs in your area. Some libraries have even started programs where gardeners can donate collected seed or "check out" packets of seeds to grow in their home gardens.

Seeds collected from your garden can make great gifts, like these bean seeds that were offered as a baby-shower favor.

Collecting Tree Nuts

If you're willing to give up the instant gratification of buying an established tree, growing trees from local seed is a terrific way to provide wildlife habitat and food. But is planting trees from seed as easy as dropping a nut in the ground? If blue jays and squirrels can do it, it can't be that hard, right? While planting trees from seed isn't terribly difficult, there are some things to consider if you want the best results.

Begin by selecting mature nuts from healthy trees in your area. Gather nuts that have fallen naturally, ensuring that they are fully developed and free from damage. Be sure to check for small holes, which may indicate that the nut has already provided a home for hungry insects, like acorn weevils.

With some species of seed, including acorns, hickory nuts, and walnuts, you can conduct a float test to determine viability. Simply toss collected nuts into a bucket of water for several minutes. For nuts with outer shells, like hickories and walnuts, you'll want to remove the hull before performing the float test. Anything that floats should be discarded, as floating nuts indicate too much air, which was likely caused by pests or disease. Perform the float test shortly after harvesting, as waiting too long can cause viable nuts to dry out, increasing the likelihood that they'll float.

Once you've determined viability of seeds, you can remove any outer shells or husks, taking care not to damage the inner nut. Depending on the species, you may need to soak the nuts in water, which will soften the shells and promote germination. After soaking, carefully remove any remaining outer layers. Before planting, seeds should be stratified, a technique that simulates natural conditions and improves germination rates. To stratify, place the nuts in moist soil or sand and store in a refrigerator for several months. Ensure that the nuts are kept moist during this time. This process of stratification imitates the natural winter dormancy period for seeds, encouraging a better chance at sprouting. When spring arrives and you're ready to plant, choose a suitable location, ensuring that it provides ideal space and growing conditions for the species. Prepare the soil

Tree nuts with small chew holes can be an indicator that the nut served as a cozy home for an insect, like this acorn weevil, which will render the seed unviable. ↑

by loosening it and amending it with organic matter to promote healthy root development, and provide consistent watering to support germination and initial growth.

Seed Storage and Management

As you gather seeds from native plants or your vegetable garden, it's essential to keep detailed records of the species, location, and date of collection. This information will help you to track the origins of your seeds and ensure that you know what seeds you have on hand. Label each batch of seeds clearly and accurately, including both the common and scientific names of the plant, collection date, and any relevant notes about the plant's characteristics. Adopting a system that provides consistency in labeling will help you easily identify seeds when it's time to plant them.

Proper storage conditions are also important for preserving seed viability. Store seeds in a cool, dry, and dark place to prevent moisture buildup and prevent the growth of mold or fungus. Use airtight containers, glass jars, or resealable plastic bags to protect seeds from humidity. Adding desiccant packets to containers can prevent excess moisture buildup that could lead to spoiled seeds. For long-term storage, store seeds in the refrigerator or freezer, especially if you plan to save them for multiple growing seasons. Just be sure to check stored seeds regularly for signs of moisture or damage and remove seeds at the first sign of issues to prevent problems from spreading to other seeds.

COLLECT ETHICALLY

As interest in native plant gardening grows, so do concerns about unethical propagation of native species. When collecting native plant seeds for your own garden, always prioritize the well-being of natural ecosystems and nature preserves. If you're collecting seed from outside of your own property, always get permission from landowners or relevant authorities. Focus on collecting from areas where seeds are abundant, and only collect a small portion of seeds from any given population to ensure that local populations of native plants continue to thrive. Avoid collecting seeds from protected areas, such as nature preserves or national parks, as disrupting protected areas can have detrimental impacts on local flora and fauna and collection of seed may be illegal. Instead, look for opportunities to collect from non-protected areas, such as your own garden or the gardens of friends and neighbors.

Avoid collecting seed from protected natural areas, like national parks or nature preserves.

Chapter 16

MAKE THE MOST OF COMPOST

Every year, a staggering 40 percent of all food in the United States is wasted, and much of that waste ends up rotting in landfills. Food waste accounts for nearly 25 percent of all waste sent to the dump, and this wasteful practice isn't confined to the act of discarding leftovers; it stretches across the entire food supply chain, from farm to fork. Vast fields of perfectly good produce are left unharvested, often rejected for size, shape, or color. Supermarkets discard items that have reached their sell-by dates, despite much of this food being safe to eat. And households contribute to this growing dilemma by tossing produce that was purchased as a performative act of eating healthier but was instead forgotten in the back of the refrigerator as cravings for fast food won over (it happens to the best of us).

The consequences of food waste extend far beyond the copious amounts of untouched produce sent to the landfill each year. Scarce resources like water, energy, and arable land are squandered in the production of food that never reaches a dinner plate. The Environmental Protection Agency estimates that food loss and waste accounts for 170 million metric tons of carbon dioxide equivalent greenhouse gas emissions every year, an amount equal to the yearly CO_2 emissions of 42 coal-fired power plants. Even worse, these emissions don't include the decomposition of food waste in landfills, which releases methane, a potent greenhouse gas that accelerates climate change.

Turning Waste to Wealth

Home composting won't solve the problem of food waste entirely, but channeling overripe or rotten produce, kitchen scraps, yard clippings, and discarded paper products into a compost pile can alleviate the amount of waste that ends up rotting in landfills. What emerges from this transformative process is a nutrient-dense substance known to many as black gold, the perfect ingredient for cultivating healthier, more productive gardens. Compost can be used to enhance soil structure, moisture retention, and nutrient availability for all those wonderful native plants in your wildlife garden or those veggies and herbs in your food garden.

At the heart of composting lies decomposition, a natural process orchestrated by a myriad of microorganisms that perform the task of breaking down organic matter. Composting begins with a hidden diversity of bacteria, fungi, and other microscopic soil-dwelling creatures that feast on leaves, kitchen scraps, and yard waste, collectively transforming organic matter into smaller and simpler substances. As microorganisms break down materials, they free essential nutrients and carbon that will later nourish the garden.

smelly compost pile that attracts pests. Maintaining this balance involves consistently adding a variety of both carbon-rich and nitrogen-rich materials to your compost pile. As kitchen scraps and green materials are added, they should be interspersed with dry leaves, straw, or other carbon sources.

There are a few things you should avoid throwing in the compost bin. Meat, dairy, and

Creating the Perfect Compost Recipe

Achieving the right balance between carbon-rich (brown) and nitrogen-rich (green) materials is one of the most important aspects of successful composting. Carbon-rich materials like dry leaves and wood chips provide the energy source that microorganisms need for their metabolic processes. These materials also help create the ideal structure that allows for adequate airflow and prevents the compost pile from becoming too compacted. Nitrogen-rich materials including kitchen scraps, grass clippings, and coffee grounds provide essential nutrients like protein that microorganisms need to function efficiently.

The optimal ratio of carbon to nitrogen in a compost pile is typically around 30:1, or 30 parts carbon for each part nitrogen, though this can vary slightly depending on the specific materials used. A balanced mixture of both types of materials ensures that microorganisms have the necessary energy and nutrients to carry out the decomposition process. Too much carbon-rich material can result in slow decomposition, as microorganisms lack the nitrogen required for growth and activity. Conversely, an excess of nitrogen-rich materials can lead to a slimy and

Mind Your Mix: What to Include in Your Compost Pile

Green (Nitrogen-Rich) Materials	Brown (Carbon-Rich) Materials
Fruit scraps	Fallen leaves
Vegetable scraps	Shredded newspaper and cardboard
Coffee grounds	Wood chips and sawdust
Tea bags that do not contain plastic (check by brand and remove staples)	Unwaxed paper plates and napkins
Grass clippings	Unbleached paper towels
Disease-free plant trimmings and weeds	Pine needles
	Straw

oily foods should not be composted, as they can attract pests. Additionally, pet waste and treated wood should be excluded due to the potential presence of harmful pathogens or chemicals. Diseased plants, invasive weeds, and materials treated with pesticides should also be kept out of the compost, as they may not fully break down or could introduce unwanted elements into the soil. While eggshells add negligible amounts of carbon and nitrogen to the compost, they are a good source of calcium and can be washed and crushed before composting.

Fallen leaves make a great addition to the compost pile, adding carbon-rich resources that can help balance out nitrogen-rich food scraps. ↑

Kitchen scraps, like fruit and vegetable peels, add nitrogen to compost. →

Building Your Compost System

There's no one right way to construct a home compost system. The choice between DIY compost receptacles and plastic tumbler-style bins boils down to personal preference, space, budget, and composting goals. While DIY bins offer customization and cost savings, tumbler bins provide convenience and improved aeration. The key is to select a composting method that aligns with your needs.

If you're producing a lot of food and yard waste and love a good DIY project, consider building your own compost bin. One of the most significant benefits of DIY bins is their cost-effectiveness, as bins can be crafted from materials like wood pallets, wire mesh, cinder blocks, or other materials that you may have readily available or can find cheaply. You can also use something as simple as a large plastic tote if you're aiming to keep your composting goals small. DIY bins are also highly customizable in size, allowing you to tailor the bin to fit your available space and composting needs.

There are some drawbacks to consider if you're planning to build your own bin. DIY bins need to be manually turned to maintain proper aeration. A bin left unturned will lack oxygen, leading to slower decomposition and potential odor issues. If the bin has an open design, it may also attract pests like rodents and raccoons.

Commercially available plastic tumbler-style compost bins offer a different approach. These bins are designed with convenience and efficiency in mind. One of their main advantages is improved aeration and mixing thanks to their tumbling mechanism, which provides better

airflow and faster decomposition. Additionally, the enclosed design of tumbler bins serves as a barrier against pests, preventing unwanted scavenging. These bins are also neat and compact, making them ideal for small spaces. Despite their advantages, plastic tumbler-style bins come with their own set of drawbacks. They tend to be more expensive upfront compared to DIY options, and while they offer efficient turning, their fixed capacity might be too limiting if you have heftier composting needs.

Maintain Your Compost

A well-tended compost pile can become a thriving habitat for countless microorganisms that work together to break down organic materials. As you nurture your compost, consider it a dynamic ecosystem that demands ongoing attention and care. After all, there are many factors that work in harmony to transform organic materials into nutrient-rich compost.

Like you, compost needs oxygen. Oxygen fuels the activities of aerobic bacteria, which are essential for efficient decomposition. You can ensure that your compost receives the oxygen it needs by routinely turning the mix. Regular turning will also prevent compaction, which inhibits airflow and hinders the breakdown process. If you have a rotating bin, simply rotate it a few times whenever you add new materials.

Monitoring the temperature of your compost can also provide insights into the rate of decomposition. As microorganisms break down organic matter, they generate heat as a byproduct. A higher internal temperature indicates that the microbial activity is thriving, and the pile is actively breaking down. But it's important to

FROM TOP
Consider collecting kitchen scraps in a small, enclosed pail that you can empty into your outdoor compost bin when full.

Tumbler-style compost bins make turning the mix a breeze.

This large DIY compost bin was constructed with leftover wood and concrete blocks.

Vermicomposting is a practice that involves using worms to break down organic waste. The process relies on a specific type of earthworm, typically red wigglers, which are known for their voracious appetite and ability to transform organic matter into valuable compost. While vermicomposting is a popular way to handle organic food waste, there are some considerations you should keep in mind. Proper maintenance is crucial to ensure worm health and composting efficiency. Maintaining the right moisture levels and providing adequate aeration is essential, as worms require a specific environment to thrive. Overfeeding your worms can lead to a buildup of organic matter, causing odors and attracting unwanted pests.

Another major concern associated with vermicomposting is the risk of worms escaping and becoming invasive. While red wigglers are highly effective at breaking down organic matter, their hardiness and adaptability could lead to them thriving in non-native environments. If vermicomposting is practiced outdoors in regions where these worms are not native, there is a risk that they could establish themselves in the wild and potentially disrupt local ecosystems. To mitigate this risk, it's recommended to vermicompost indoors or within controlled environments.

strike a balance—excessively high temperatures could kill off beneficial microorganisms, affecting the overall health of the compost.

Proper moisture levels are also important for successful composting. Your compost pile should be as damp as a wrung-out sponge. Too much moisture can lead to anaerobic conditions and unpleasant odors, while too little moisture can slow down decomposition. Moisture content directly influences microbial activity, as bacteria and other decomposers need water to carry out their work effectively. Regularly checking the moisture level and adjusting as needed is essential in maintaining optimal compost conditions. A quick spray with the hose can increase moisture, while covering your compost before expected rainfall can prevent excessive saturation.

Overcome Compost Conundrums

Composting is a learning journey, and each challenge you encounter presents an opportunity to fine-tune your approach. Troubleshooting common issues not only improves your composting skills but also deepens your connection to the natural processes at play in

your backyard ecosystem. Here are a few help-ful tips that might help you overcome common compost problems.

Foul odors emanating from the compost pile are usually an indication of improper aera-tion or excessive moisture. To remedy this, give the pile a good turn to introduce oxygen and improve airflow. Ensure that you're not adding too much wet or nitrogen-rich material without balancing it with dry, carbon-rich material. If the compost appears sluggish in its decomposi-tion journey, it may need more nitrogen, which is essential for the activity of bacteria. Adding green materials like kitchen scraps or grass clippings can help reignite microbial action.

Flies, while expected inhabitants of the com-post pile, can sometimes become overwhelming.

Fruit flies in particular are attracted to rotting food scraps. To mitigate their presence, bury kitchen scraps beneath a layer of brown mate-rial and avoid letting food waste sit on top of the pile. Routine turning of the pile can also disrupt the fly breeding cycle and reduce their population. If flies persist, cover the pile with a layer of fine mesh or screening to prevent their entry while still allowing airflow.

Routine turning of the compost pile will ensure the mix receives the oxy-gen it needs to decompose.

PASS ON THE PEAT

· ·

Since the mid-1900s, peat moss has been a popular growing medium in the garden thanks to its ability to retain moisture without becoming waterlogged. But the use of peat moss in gardening has significant environmental implications. As the name implies, peat moss comes from peat bogs, unique wetland ecosystems that accumulate organic matter over thousands of years. Like all wetland habitats, peat bogs are carbon sinks. In fact, peatlands store one-third of the world's carbon. But when peat moss is harvested from these bogs, all the carbon that has been sequestered and stored for thousands of years is released into the atmosphere, contributing to climate change. In addition to the release of carbon, the harvesting of peat bogs for peat moss also destroys critical habitat for a diversity of rare and endangered plant and animal species, many of which are uniquely adapted to these wetland environments.

When choosing a growing medium for the garden, it's best to pass on peat moss mixes. Instead, choose options that rely on renewable resources like bark or wood fiber, coconut coir, or leaf mulch. Better yet, start your own compost pile and create black gold right in your own backyard. This simple choice not only reduces carbon emissions but also helps safeguard vulnerable ecosystems and promotes a more sustainable approach to gardening.

· ·

Peat bogs store carbon and provide habitat for countless species of wildlife.

GUILT-FREE GARDENING

· ·

Composting is a practical way to redirect waste that would otherwise end up rotting in a landfill. But there are other ways you can reduce the amount of trash your gardening activities produce. Avoid single-use plastics whenever possible. With many garden centers selling commercial plants in plastic pots, this can sometimes be unavoidable. More local nurseries are opting for compostable pots, which are plastic-free, biodegradable, and made from materials like composted cow manure. These pots can be planted directly in the garden, giving your plants a great start to life by providing essential nutrients as the pots decompose and release nutrients into the soil. If you do find yourself with an abundance of plastic pots, find ways to reuse them (like growing new plants with the seeds you

collect from your garden) or drop them at a garden center that offers a recycling program specifically designed for plant pots.

· ·

FROM TOP

Gardening can generate a lot of plastic waste, but many of these small pots can be recycled or reused for growing new plants.

These pots are made from composted cow manure and offer a sustainable alternative to traditional plastic pots.

Chapter 17

FORGE COMMUNITY UNITY

In suburban and urban neighborhoods, where gardens are extensions of homes, the creation of wildlife-friendly spaces can often cause concern about curb appeal. The idea of wild expanses of untamed growth in a home landscape might raise eyebrows among neighbors who cherish manicured lawns and neatly trimmed hedges. Won't wildlife gardens attract rodents and snakes? Will ticks become a problem? Will a wild garden decrease property values or have a negative impact on the neighborhood? Could a wildlife garden create a breeding ground for disease-carrying insects like mosquitoes? Ultimately, there lies a delicate balance between cultivating habitats for wildlife and respecting neighborhood expectations.

Keep It Tidy

Creating wildlife gardens that align with neighborhood expectations requires a thoughtful approach. While natural and untamed gardens may appear charming to some, to others they risk community reputation. Fortunately, there are practical ways to keep your garden looking

tidy without compromising the ecological benefits it provides. Consideration should be given to the layout, design, and selection of native plants so that your garden not only provides habitat and sustenance for wildlife but also blends seamlessly within your community. Incorporating elements of structure such as neatly defined borders or designated pathways can further help ease concerns about your landscape appearing unkempt.

Create Neat and Neighborly Edges

Neat and well-defined garden edges not only enhance the overall visual appeal of your wildlife garden, they play an important role in addressing concerns that your neighbors might have about the perceived tidiness of your landscape. By creating clear boundaries between the highly cultivated areas of your landscape (like turfgrass) and gardens that are more natural in form and function, you can ensure that wildlife habitats remain distinct and intentional. Neat borders serve as a powerful visual representation of the

deliberate effort to balance ecological conservation and aesthetic appeal, showcasing how wildlife-friendly gardens can seamlessly coexist with your community's aesthetic.

Garden borders can further reinforce the overall look and feel of your landscape. For instance, using rocks or branches that blur the line between garden and habitat can establish a more naturalistic feel to your garden, whereas materials like cut stone can create structured edges with obvious intent and a more traditional look. There's no right or wrong answer, and you might opt for a "mullet" approach where your front yard is kept neat and tidy, but the backyard has a bit of a wilder side. No matter the materials or approach you choose, borders not only delineate spaces but also add a natural and visually appealing element to the landscape.

By using spades or specialized edging shears, you can emphasize intentionality by maintaining clean lines and preventing the encroachment of plants beyond designated borders. For a more subtle and seamless look, you might go for plant-based edges, utilizing low-growing, compact plants like border grasses, groundcovers, or flowering perennials to define your garden's edges. This not only adds to the overall beauty of the garden but also serves as a practical way to create boundaries while encouraging biodiversity. The choice of edging materials can be tailored to match your style, whether it's formal or informal. The goal is to ensure that the edges of the wildlife garden are distinct, well-maintained, and fully integrated into the surrounding environment, addressing any neighborly concerns about neatness.

FROM TOP

Stone borders can provide a formal touch to a native garden.

....

Log borders maintain a more naturalistic feel in a native garden.

....

Garden edges can be kept neat and tidy with a variety of natural or constructed materials.

....

KEEP IT SAFE

. . . .

While lazy landscaping can help support wildlife, it's always a good idea to keep an eye out for hazards that might arise from taking a more laissez-faire approach to landscaping. Be sure to trim overgrown plants, clear debris, and keep paths and walkways accessible so your garden doesn't pose a safety risk to neighbors and passersby. Also keep an eye on the canopy. If you have large trees on your property, make a point to visually inspect them for any broken or hanging branches that could pose a safety risk should they fall.

. . . .

If you're keen to leave your leaves in your yard, be sure to keep sidewalks and other public areas clear.

Designate Areas for Compost Bins and Brush Piles

Compost bins and brush piles aren't the most attractive parts of a wildlife garden. Rather than have these elements front and center in your home landscape, create a designated space where the neighbors aren't forced to look at them every day. Compost bins can be placed discreetly behind hedgerows or concealed by native plant gardens or small fences. Similarly, brush piles can be organized and situated under the canopy of larger trees or tucked into an inconspicuous corner of the yard. Avoid placing piles too close to your home to keep wildlife from nesting near or under your home's foundation or structures like decks.

Mulch Your Beds

There are loads of benefits to incorporating mulch into your garden beds and pollinator patches. Mulch provides a uniform and tidy appearance to your garden and creates defined borders and pathways, which allows you to keep things neighborly by providing a polished look to your wildlife garden. But the benefits don't stop there. Mulch can also help suppress weeds and create a moisture barrier and soil insulator, eliminating the need for chemical herbicides while reducing the need for watering.

Design with Intent

Be strategic in your selection and placement of plants. Placing lower-growing plants at the front of garden beds and reserving taller species for the back ensures that plants do not obstruct sidewalks, pathways, or other public areas. This design choice also prevents taller plants from overshadowing or crowding out their smaller companions, ensuring that all species receive adequate sunlight and space to thrive. If you notice your plants encroaching on your neighbor's property, be proactive about addressing neighborly concerns. Some neighbors might welcome the addition of wildlife-friendly plants on their property, while others might just as soon erect a fence to avoid having perceived weeds trespass on their grass.

Ticked about Ticks

If you're cultivating a landscape for wildlife, you might run into concerns about increased prevalence of ticks in your neighborhood. Ticks can indeed be a concern, especially in regions of the world where they are common like the central and eastern United States. Clearing away tall grasses and leaf litter near gathering spaces, walkways, and play areas can help minimize tick habitat and reduce the likelihood of exposure.

In areas that might be suitable for ticks, create a border of wood chips, gravel, or mulch

Be sure to monitor the growth of native plants to ensure they don't encroach on public sidewalks or a neighbor's property.

Deer tick

CREATE TICK TUBES

DIY tick tubes are a proactive and nature-friendly way to help prevent ticks from proliferating in your home landscape. These tubes are designed to target ticks in their larval or nymph life stages by using insecticide-treated nesting materials that are attractive to mice, which are common hosts for young ticks. The idea is to treat the nesting material with a tick-killing insecticide, which mice then collect and bring back to their nests, effectively eliminating ticks present in those nests. This approach reduces the reliance on broad-spectrum chemical pesticides and minimizes the risk to other wildlife.

DIY tick tubes can be made using simple materials such as toilet paper tubes and permethrin-treated cotton balls or dryer lint. Placing tubes in areas frequented by mice, such as along the edges of your property or in natural hiding spots, can help decrease tick populations without harming other wildlife, creating a safer outdoor environment for your family and neighbors.

DIY tick tubes can help lessen your chance of tick exposure in your wildlife garden.

between the garden and the lawn to serve as a natural barrier. Regularly maintaining the landscape by trimming shrubs and trees and keeping the grass short in well-traversed areas can help deter ticks from lingering in the garden. Choosing plants that are not attractive to deer, which are often carriers of ticks, can further reduce the risk.

If you do happen to notice ticks becoming a problem, educate yourself and your family on how to prevent exposure. Dress in long sleeves and pants. Tuck your pants into your socks and your shirt into your pants so ticks don't have easy access to skin. Before heading indoors, use a lint roller to pick up any stray ticks lingering on your clothing. Once inside, toss your clothes in the dryer on the hottest setting for at least six minutes to kill any ticks. Finally, be sure to perform a thorough tick check before hitting the shower. All members of your family (pets included) should be checked. Pay particular attention to crevices and scalps, where ticks love to hide.

Symbols of Sanctuary

Certifying your garden as wildlife habitat makes a statement about the intent of your landscape. It's like planting a flag of commitment to conservation, and it can serve as a powerful proclamation that not only reflects your dedication to creating a thriving habitat for local wildlife but also serves as inspiration for others to follow suit. Many certifications come with recognition, often in the form of a yard sign that you can proudly display. Certifying through the National Wildlife Federation's Certified Wildlife Habitat program, for instance, allows you to publicly promote your garden as an official haven for wildlife. Some local governments and community associations also offer certifications for nature-friendly yards.

Here are a few more national certification programs that provide symbols of sanctuary that you can display in your garden.

→ → → → → → → → → → → → → → → →

Monarch Waystation

The Monarch Waystation program, offered through Monarch Watch, is an initiative that encourages individuals and communities to make a meaningful contribution to monarch butterfly conservation. From habitat loss to climate change, monarchs face many challenges. But designing waystations with milkweed, the host plant for monarch caterpillars, and nectar-rich flowers to nourish adult butterflies can help in providing the resources they need to make their long migrations each year. By certifying your waystation, you'll join a network of dedicated conservationists committed to preserving monarchs and their extraordinary journey.

Certified Firefly Habitat

The Certified Firefly Habitat program, hosted by the non-profit organization Firefly Conservation and Research, is an initiative that encourages individuals to take an active role in preserving firefly populations. By certifying your landscape as a firefly-friendly habitat, you'll commit to creating a welcoming environment for these bioluminescent insects in your own backyard. The organization's website provides resources and guidelines needed to make your outdoor space more firefly friendly, which includes practices like reducing light pollution, minimizing pesticide use, and planting native vegetation.

Pollinator Habitat

Renowned for their research and education on pollinator conservation, the Xerces Society offers a Pollinator Habitat sign to help wildlife gardeners show their dedication to the cause. This sign serves as a powerful statement for anyone who dedicates space to pollinator-friendly plants and practices, including a commitment to not using pesticides. It also signifies that your garden is a place of intentionality, staving off those who might be interested in mowing areas that are meant to be kept intact for bees, butterflies, and other pollinating insects.

COMMUNICATION IS KEY

If you're on talking terms with your neighbors, engaging in open and respectful conversations is a valuable step in alleviating any concerns they might have about your wildlife garden. Emphasize the benefits that your garden provides for pollinators, birds, and other wildlife by sharing your passion for creating a vibrant and ecologically diverse habitat that supports not only local wildlife but the community as a whole. Address concerns about tidiness or potential pest issues by explaining your plans for managing your garden's appearance and addressing any potential challenges. Inviting neighbors to participate in gardening workshops or events and sharing educational resources can also foster a sense of belonging and involvement, empowering neighbors to enact change at home and assuring them that your intentions are environmentally conscious as well as community focused. You can even share seeds, plants, or produce from your garden so they too can reap the benefits of your efforts. By fostering open lines of communication and showcasing the positive aspects of your wildlife garden, you can help put your neighbors' worries at ease and cultivate a sense of understanding and support for your garden.

Chapter 18

BECOME A BACKYARD SCIENTIST

All around the world, scientists and researchers are busy collecting and interpreting data about the natural world. Unfortunately, there simply aren't enough scientists in the world to observe and monitor all the various species of plants, animals, and ecosystem interactions across the planet. That's where community science can help. Community science allows researchers to scale their efforts by inviting members of the community to lend a helping hand in data collection and interpretation. With the help of volunteers from around the world, researchers can gather more data, analyze it more quickly, and make more accurate predictions about the future.

What Is Community Science?

Community science involves regular people working together with scientists to collect and analyze data that can help answer important questions about the natural world. Whether it's tracking bird populations or counting the number of fireflies in your backyard, there are countless ways to get involved. And the best part? You don't need a fancy degree or years of

training to participate. By joining a community science program, you can help contribute to scientific research in a meaningful way, and it's a wonderful excuse to play outside, learn new skills, and connect with other people who share your passion for nature and wildlife.

Community Science from Your Own Backyard

With a variety of community science programs available to participate in, seasoned scientists and curious newbies alike are sure to find ways to get involved. Here are a few programs that you can join from the comfort of your own backyard.

Journey North

Managed by the University of Wisconsin–Madison Arboretum, Journey North is a community science program that invites people to monitor seasonal biological events and submit their observations via an online portal. The program offers a diversity of projects including tracking monarch butterflies, hummingbirds,

Participating in community science is a fun way to get the family excited about gardening for wildlife.

red-winged blackbirds, annual leaf-out of trees, and many more. Scientists use the data collected to better understand the migration and movement of wildlife and how changes in climate and habitat impact them. Journey North provides a range of resources to help people get started so professional researchers and casual observers alike will feel welcome to participate.

Monarch Watch

Based at the University of Kansas, Monarch Watch has emerged as a leader in community science initiatives, engaging volunteers in the study and protection of monarch butterflies and their habitats. At the core of Monarch Watch's mission is the tagging program, where volunteers affix small, uniquely coded tags to the wings of monarch butterflies before their migration to overwintering sites in Mexico. This tagging effort has provided invaluable data on monarch migration patterns, contributing significantly to the understanding of the species' complex life cycle and the factors influencing their population dynamics. Monarch Watch has also been instrumental in promoting the planting of milkweed—the sole host plant for

COMMUNITY SCIENCE vs. CITIZEN SCIENCE

· ·

When it comes to involving the public in scientific research, two terms are often used interchangeably: community science and citizen science. At their core, both community science and citizen science involve engaging non-scientists in the scientific process. The goal is to tap into the knowledge, skills, and curiosity of community members, and to use that collective power to create a better understanding of how the world works.

So, what's the difference between community science and citizen science? Citizen science generally implies a top-down approach in which professional scientists or institutions invite the public to help with their research. This can often exclude marginalized communities who may not see themselves as "citizens" in a traditional sense. Conversely, community science emphasizes a more grassroots approach in which the community is the driving force behind the research. This can be especially important for ensuring that underrepresented communities have a voice in the scientific process.

By using more inclusive language, community science can help break down barriers and build trust between scientists and the public. After all, embracing a diversity of perspectives and knowledge is fundamental to creating solutions to complex problems like climate change and biodiversity loss.

· ·

Journey North tracks a variety of migratory species, like this ruby-throated hummingbird.

CLOCKWISE
Monarch Watch is a
community science
program dedicated to
tracking populations of
monarch butterflies.

The Great Backyard
Bird Count encourages
volunteers to track bird
species from their own
yards and communities.

Volunteers tag a mon-
arch butterfly.

monarch larvae—and nectar-rich flowers to cre-ate essential habitats for monarchs throughout their migration routes. Get started by planting your own monarch waystation, reporting obser-vations of tagged monarchs, or participating in the tagging program.

The Great Backyard Bird Count

Hosted by the Cornell Lab of Ornithology and National Audubon Society, the Great Backyard Bird Count is a four-day community science event that takes place every February with the goal of observing as many birds as possi-ble. All skill levels are welcome to join in the birdwatching fun. Simply select a location to observe birds for at least 15 minutes and iden-tify as many birds as you can see or hear. Then, submit your observations online. Not great with bird identification? No problem—mobile apps like Merlin Bird ID can help. Scientists use the data collected during the Great Backyard Bird Count to monitor changes in bird populations and track the spread of diseases that impact birds. This information is crucial for develop-ing conservation strategies and protecting the habitats that birds depend upon.

The Lost Ladybug Project

Ladybugs, also called lady beetles or ladybird beetles, are important predatory insects. Unfor-tunately, many native ladybug species are in decline due to habitat loss, pesticide use, and competition from non-native species. The Lost Ladybug Project hosted by Cornell University engages the public in finding and photograph-ing native ladybugs to better understand their distribution in North America. Community members are invited to photograph ladybugs that they find in their home gardens and other outdoor spaces and upload them to the Lost Ladybug Project website. The photos are then

analyzed by a team of scientists who use them to track the distribution and population trends of different ladybug species. Visit the Lost Ladybug Project's website for instructions on how to take and submit photos, as well as information on how to identify different species of ladybugs.

Project Budburst

Managed by the Chicago Botanic Garden, Budburst invites participants to observe the life cycle of various plant species and report on events including first leaves, first flowers, and seed dispersal. By tracking the timing of plant life cycle phases, you can help researchers better understand how plants respond to seasonal fluctuations. Over time, these observations can help scientists piece together how climate change affects plants and the pollinators that depend on them for survival. To get started, create an account on the Budburst website and choose a plant to observe from the available list. The website provides a list of common plants and when each species typically buds, flowers, and produces seeds. Participants are encouraged to submit observations from their home gardens, neighborhoods, parks, or any other location with plants.

FROM TOP
Polished lady beetle on
goldenrod

Butterfly milkweed

PHENOLOGY: NATURE'S CALENDAR

In nature, timing is everything. Plants and animals rely on environmental cues like temperature and daylight to time important cyclical life events like flowering, leaf-out, migration, and emergence. This is phenology, the study of the timing of natural phenomena and the synchrony between living organisms and their environment. Community science programs are helping track how phenological phenomena are shifting over time, providing valuable clues to how climate change is altering the behavior of some species and how plants and animals are adapting—or failing to adapt—to a warming world. These observations can inform conservation strategies in the face of ongoing environmental changes.

Project FeederWatch

Operated by the Cornell Lab of Ornithology and Birds Canada, Project FeederWatch is a community science program that aims to track bird populations, as well as mammals, throughout winter across North America. By volunteering to observe backyard avian visitors, you can help scientists monitor long-term trends in bird populations and better understand the distribution and abundance of various species. Participating in Project FeederWatch is easy and requires no formal training or expertise. All you need is an area of your yard with bird feeders or plantings that you maintain for birds, a bird identification guide, and the ability to spend a few minutes each week watching and counting the birds and mammals that visit your yard. Visit the Project FeederWatch website to sign up. You'll receive a research kit that includes a bird identification poster and instructions on how to record your observations. Once you start observing, you can submit your data online and help contribute to a valuable database of bird populations.

Chickadee at feeder

Bumble Bee Atlas

The Bumble Bee Atlas is a collaboration between Xerces Society scientists, state and federal agency biologists, university scientists, and volunteers you who are interested in collecting data on bumble bees in North America. The program invites people of all ages and experience levels to participate by observing and reporting bumble bee sightings in their local area. Researchers use the data to create distribution maps of bumble bee species and monitor population changes over time. To get started, visit the Bumble Bee Atlas website to see if there is an active program in your area. The program asks participants to attend a training workshop and conduct at least two surveys during a specific sampling window. Don't have an active Bumble Bee Atlas project in your state or region? You can still contribute to bumble bee research by submitting observations to Bumble Bee Watch.

Firefly Watch

If you love watching fireflies light up your garden on summer evenings, Firefly Watch could be the perfect opportunity to get involved with community science. In response to the recent decline of these bioluminescent insects, Mass Audubon created Firefly Watch as a way for people to observe and report firefly sightings from their own backyard or community. This data helps researchers better understand firefly populations, habitat, and behavior across North America. Get started by registering on the Mass Audubon website and following the guidelines to collect and submit your observations. The program only requires about ten minutes per week, and you don't need any fancy equipment or skills, making it fun and accessible for the whole family.

FROM LEFT

Eastern bumble bee on a
purple coneflower

Participating in Firefly
Watch can help scientists
track declines in firefly
populations.

New Era of Science

Too much screen time can be a bad thing, but what if that screen time was spent collecting data that scientists might one day use to make a scientific breakthrough? Nearly 80 percent of the world's population use smartphones. The accessibility of this kind of technology has opened community science to a wider audience, including those who may not have had access to specialized equipment or training in the past. Now, with a smartphone in hand, a community scientist can easily snap photos, record observations, and upload data to online platforms for analysis, helping democratize scientific research and engage average people in the study and protection of nature and wildlife.

iNaturalist

Whether you're a gardener, nature enthusiast, or someone who simply loves spending time outdoors, iNaturalist is a great way to learn more about the diversity of life on Earth. The platform brings together a network of community scientists and researchers under a common mission: build a global community of 100 million naturalists by 2030 in order to connect people to nature and advance biodiversity science and conservation. By inviting people to share photographs of plants and animals they observe in their community, scientists can use the data that community members collect to better understand the diversity of life on our planet and how biodiversity is globally distributed. To

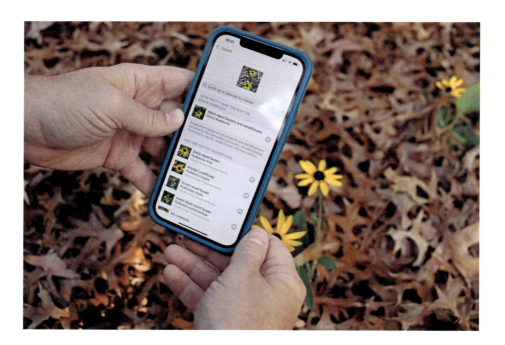

iNaturalist, which invites volunteers to share photos of the plants and animals they observe, hopes to build a community of 100 million naturalists.

get started, you'll need a smartphone or a digital camera to take photos of the plants, animals, and other organisms you see in your backyard or neighborhood. After you snap a photo, upload it to the iNaturalist website or app. From there, the platform's network of scientists, researchers, and other experts will help identify the plants and animals you've found.

Community Science Fosters Equity

With more than half of the world's population living in cities, inviting urbanites into the conservation conversation is increasingly important. Community science programs foster equity in scientific discovery by encouraging anyone—even those living in cities—to contribute to conservation research, regardless of their level of education or professional background. The City Nature Challenge, which has grown rapidly since its inception in 2016, encourages people to observe and document plants and wildlife in the city. In 2023, more than 66,000 people participated in the bioblitz-style event, garnering more than 1.8 million species observations in urban areas around the world.

Community science projects centered in urban areas can also help address environmental injustices, such as the unequal distribution of air and water pollution and resource extraction. By involving community members in the research process, scientists can gain a better understanding of the environmental challenges faced by communities that have been historically underrepresented in conservation and work with those communities to develop effective solutions.

Chapter 19

FIND TIME FOR REST AND PLAY

From our televisions and smart phones to our computers and even our cars, screens dominate the world in which we live. As the world becomes ever more digitally connected, it's easy to forget the importance—and joy—of spending time in nature. According to a study conducted by "The Nature of Americans," more than 50 percent of adults report spending fewer than five hours per week outdoors. What's more, most adults were content with this meager amount of time spent outside. The same study revealed that children aged eight to twelve spend three times as many hours each week glued to electronic devices such as computers and televisions than they do playing outdoors. So, what's the solution? Get outside!

Nature Is Nurturing

In our fast-paced world, stress is a constant companion—or more like a toxic friend—for many people. Over time, chronic stress can have serious consequences for your mental and physical well-being. But stepping outside can help reduce levels of cortisol, the hormone associated with stress, and promote relaxation.

Spending time outdoors
can elevate your mood and
help restore healthy sleeping patterns.

Time in nature has been linked to improved mood and reduced symptoms of depression and anxiety, likely due to the fact that being in nature encourages physical activity, which has been shown to increase endorphins and other "feel-good" chemicals in the brain. Spending time in nature can also help you catch up on that much-needed beauty rest. Soaking in some sunlight and fresh air during the day can help regulate your body's circadian rhythms, leading to a better night's rest. In fact, just one weekend getaway in nature is enough to reset your body's internal clock and improve sleep for weeks to come (Stothard et al., 2017). With as many as 70 million Americans suffering from disordered sleeping, a little time in nature might be just what the doctor ordered. If you're gardening with nature and wildlife in mind, chances are you won't need to go too far beyond your doorstep to reap all the wonderful benefits that nature has to offer.

Create a Nature Nook

As you create an oasis for wildlife at home, don't forget to nourish your own needs too. From raking and weeding to planting and harvesting, it's all too easy to make your time outdoors all work and no play. It's important to step back and soak in the beauty and bounty of your efforts. Birds build nests. Bunnies dig burrows. Beavers build lodges. You, too, should have a place where you can unwind and decompress. After all, creating a climate- and wildlife-friendly landscape can be exhausting.

As you create safe spaces for the wildlife that visit your yard, consider creating your own retreat too. This nature nook can be as simple as a comfy chair within viewing distance of a pollinator garden, or a hammock next to a small pond where you can listen to the gentle sound of trickling water. Once you've created a peaceful sanctuary, there are plenty of activities you can engage in to fully enjoy your outdoor oasis. Curl up with a good book or simply take a nap as you let the sounds of nature sing you to sleep. Regardless of how you choose to relax, spending time in your nature retreat can be restorative for the mind and body alike.

If you're looking for a deeper form of relaxation, consider meditation. Meditation can be a powerful stress-reliever, as it allows you to shift your focus from the busyness of your daily life to the peace and tranquility of your garden. The practice can also boost your mood and improve your overall well-being by making you feel more grounded and centered.

Whether it's under the shade of your favorite tree or near a trickling water feature, begin by getting comfortable and taking a few deep breaths. Inhale the fresh outdoor air and exhale any tension you're shouldering. Close your eyes and let yourself fully engage with the environment around you. Allow your senses to absorb the sights, sounds, and smells of the garden. Notice any thoughts that arise but try not to engage with them—simply let them pass. Feel the warmth of the sun on your skin or the cool breeze gently brushing against your face. Embrace the stillness and allow yourself to feel a deep sense of connection with the nature you've nurtured in your home landscape.

Cultivate Childhood Creativity and Curiosity

Outdoor play is an important part of childhood development. But not all outdoor play is created equal. Where playgrounds are prescriptive, providing visual cues for how children should interact with equipment, nature is less defined. Sticks become magical wands. Logs turn into precarious bridges over lakes of lava. And mud

FROM LEFT

A nature nook can be as simple as a chair or hammock in your favorite spot in the garden.

Outdoor play is essential for cultivating healthy minds and bodies in children.

Don't be afraid to let kids get a little dirty when playing outside.

evolves into the perfect ingredient for a delicious chocolate pie. In nature, imaginations run wild.

Nature play is an essential part of childhood development, providing numerous physical, mental, and emotional benefits for kids. Being in nature helps children develop gross motor skills as they run, climb, and jump. It also promotes hand-eye coordination as they explore and interact with their surroundings. In a world where screen time and structured activities can dominate, nature play offers an important escape for kids to simply be kids, fostering a lifelong love of the outdoors and all the wonders it holds. What's more, nature play doesn't need to be well defined. It can be as simple as digging in the dirt, searching for animal tracks, climbing trees, building forts, or simply observing plants and animals in their natural habitat.

Go on a Backyard Bug Hunt

With over one million species known to science, insects are one of the most accessible forms of wildlife on the planet. Equipped with magnifying glasses and bug catchers, young explorers can set out on a quest to discover the alien creatures that call their yard home. Don't be afraid to let them get a little dirty in the process. Encourage kids to crawl through tall grass, peek under rocks, and carefully lift leaves and logs to uncover the hidden miniature world that's lurking in the garden.

For children who are nervous around insects and spiders, start by observing some of our more charismatic and beloved bugs. Admire the colorful patterns on a butterfly's wings. Carefully catch fireflies on a warm summer evening. Or trace the formation of marching

FROM TOP
Bug-hunting can help kids overcome a fear of insects.

Catching fireflies on a warm summer evening is a memorable way to instill a love of insects in kids.

A magnifying glass can encourage kids to think like a scientist by getting them up close and personal with nature.

ants as they forage for food. For children who are more comfortable, fashion a bug catcher from an old jar or plastic container. Be sure to provide air holes and place some natural materials, like leaves and sticks, in the container so

CREATE A MUD KITCHEN

A mud kitchen is an outdoor play area for children where they can use their creativity and imagination to create sloppy soups and mucky mud pies using water, soil, and natural materials they find in your yard like sticks, leaves, flowers, and pinecones. Mud kitchens encourage kids to get outside and explore the world around them as they search for the perfect trimmings for their next recipe. Playing chef in a mud kitchen also helps kids develop their sensory and motor skills, as well as their social and emotional intelligence through collaborative play.

Building a mud kitchen doesn't have to be difficult or expensive. With just a few basic materials and some creativity, the kids in your life will be brewing and baking concoctions in no time. Your mud kitchen can be as simple or elaborate as you like. While you can purchase pre-made kitchen setups online or a from a local toy shop, building one from scratch using found materials, like logs, old pallets, scraps of wood, or even an old desk, will be far less expensive (and way more fun).

Once you've crafted your kitchen, it's time to gather utensils. Head to a local thrift shop for some pots, pans, utensils, and cups. Be sure to choose materials that can be dropped (a lot) without breaking. Metal and plastic are safer options than materials made from glass and ceramic. Don't be afraid to get creative with how you equip your kitchen. While bowls and spoons are a must, gravy boats, sieves, and muffin pans are fun options to include too.

Once your mud kitchen is fully furnished, the fun can begin. Encourage kids to experiment with different materials and mixtures, and let their imaginations soar as they create mud pies, soups, and more. You can also add in other natural materials like flowers, herbs, and even fruits and vegetables for more sensory play.

the bugs you catch feel at home. And don't forget to release all the critters you found when you're done exploring. Observing insects, spiders, and other small animals in the garden not only ignites a sense of adventure and exploration, but also nurtures a lifelong love and appreciation for the incredible diversity of life that exists just beyond your doorstep.

Nature Art

Art provides a wonderful way for children to unleash their creativity while immersing themselves in nature. Supplied with crayons, colored pencils, or paints, kids can observe and interpret the nature that surrounds them in your wildlife garden. Encourage them to find inspiration in the play of light and shadow, the textures of leaves and tree bark, the vibrant colors of flowers, or even the shapes formed in clouds. Invite them to record what they see by drawing or painting in whatever style makes them happy. Some kids will enjoy honing their skills in realism, while others may prefer to take a more abstract approach.

Perhaps creating art with natural materials is more tempting for the kids in your life. Taking inspiration from the incredible leaf arrangements of environmental artists like Andy Goldsworthy or the monochrome works of Richard Long, invite kids to find and arrange fallen leaves into colorful patterns, organize sticks or stones into awe-inspiring designs, or get downright dirty as they craft fingerpaints from mud. As you collect and use natural materials in your artwork, be sure to avoid disturbing natural habitat, and make a point to put materials back where they were found when possible. And don't forget to snap a photo so you can hang these priceless pieces in your home gallery (aka your fridge).

Encourage kids to observe differences in the shapes, sizes, colors, and even smells of leaves like these of the sassafras.

SCAVENGER HUNT

Scavenger hunts are the perfect blend of play and learning, making them an ideal outdoor activity for kids. The beauty of a successful nature scavenger hunt lies in its ability to engage all the senses and encourage children to closely observe the world around them. Begin by providing each child with a list of items or clues for things they might find in your yard or neighborhood. As you design the list of things to find, be sure to include descriptors that will have children feeling, smelling, seeing, and listening (it's best to avoid tasting). Such items could include things like a smooth pebble, a fragrant flower, a leaf with two different colors, or the call of a bird. Fully immerse their imaginations—and their senses.

A nature scavenger hunt can also provide a wonderful opportunity for children to learn about the diverse flora and fauna that inhabit their local ecosystem. Encourage them to research and identify the plants,

insects, birds, and animals they encounter during the hunt. This will not only expand their knowledge but also deepen their appreciation for backyard nature. Invite children to document their findings through sketches, photographs, or a nature journal, which will help them reflect on their experiences. Though simple, nature scavenger hunts can help children develop essential skills like problem-solving, critical thinking, and collaboration. They'll learn to follow clues, make connections, solve riddles, and work together, fueling their enthusiasm for exploring the wonders of their own backyard.

Birdwatching

From listening to barred owls call in the distance to watching bright blue robin eggs give way to hungry mouths, backyard birdwatching can jumpstart a lifelong love of nature. Kids can watch as a mother and father robin bounce around the yard, teaching a young fledgling how to find worms in the grass. Or perhaps they'll observe a cardinal taking a dip in a nearby birdbath or pond as it preens its feathers. If they're lucky, they might even catch a fleeting glimmer of a ruby-throated hummingbird as it visits a backyard hummingbird feeder. No matter the activity, birdwatching is fun for all ages.

With a simple field guide in hand, kids can learn how to recognize and identify birds by both their coloration and their calls. And you can help deepen their curiosity by providing details about bird habitats, migration patterns, and feeding habits. Beyond the thrill of spotting and identifying different species, birdwatching can foster stewardship and empathy for the natural world by encouraging children to become advocates for conservation. Invite them to help in activities like building nesting boxes for your yard or participating in community science projects that contribute valuable data to conservation efforts. You can also invite them to help with routine tasks like cleaning bird feeders and removing nests from bird boxes once they've been vacated. Encourage kids to take note of how different species use different materials and styles to construct their nests and probe their observation and critical thinking skills by asking questions about which type of nest they think is sturdier or warmer. You can even invite kids to try constructing their own nest from natural materials they find in the garden.

Chapter 20

THINK BEYOND THE BACKYARD

Many of the topics covered in this book assume three important things: 1) that you have access to a plot of land over which you have decision-making authority; 2) that your city code does not expressly prohibit gardening in ways that support nature and wildlife; and 3) that you're in a position (financial and otherwise) to prioritize nature and wildlife in your landscaping efforts. Admittedly, those are three sizable assumptions. The reality for many people is that at least one of the aforementioned things is not true.

To have a yard is to have privilege. Unfortunately, gardening for wildlife can reinforce existing inequities. The number of renters in the United States has been gradually growing over the last decade. And with each passing year, the idea of homeownership slips further out of reach for many people. As of 2023, around 34 percent of United States households were renters, representing some 115 million Americans. That's 115 million people who likely don't have the privilege of calling the shots when it comes to what types of plants are grown in the landscape, how and where harmful chemical pesticides are applied, and whether landscape decisions prioritize nature and wildlife or efficiency and tradition. Even for those who do own their own home, gardening for wildlife can be expensive and time-consuming. In some areas, it can even break the law.

To own land and to be in a position to create a thriving climate- and wildlife-friendly yard is freedom, freedom that many people may never be privileged enough to experience. We must frame our conversation around conservation within the context of the lived human experience. People across the world are facing food and employment insecurity, lack of access to basic healthcare, housing instability, systemic racism, and many more issues of social injustice. Where some people are excitedly selecting plants for a pollinator garden, others are left wondering if they can afford to feed their family today. We must approach homegrown conservation with this in mind. We must enter the conversation with empathy. And we must hold tightly the understanding that some folks simply aren't there yet, not because they do not want to be, but because they cannot be. Through all of this, we must work to ensure that those who are not privileged with land ownership are no longer burdened with the brunt of environmental impact born from poor decisions made by those who do own land.

Ideas for Building Equity

As you begin (or continue) your journey toward creating a more climate- and wildlife-friendly home landscape, here are some big ideas to consider that can expand your efforts beyond the backyard:

Check Yourself Understand your own privilege and use it to celebrate and support others. Never forget that small steps for you might be giant leaps for someone else.

Celebrate Diversity Embrace cultural diversity by incorporating traditional and Indigenous gardening practices into personal and community gardening projects.

Teach As your own expertise grows, organize community workshops and learning sessions on wildlife gardening techniques. Be sure to promote these opportunities widely.

Plant a School or Community Garden Work with community or school officials to establish gardens that allow residents without backyard spaces to participate in efforts to grow food and support wildlife.

Create Access Develop initiatives that provide resources like seeds and plants to communities interested in wildlife and food gardening.

Get Political Vote for officials who will advocate for the development of accessible green spaces in your community.

Reform Local Policy Work with city officials and policymakers to reform local landscaping regulations, allowing for more diverse and sustainable home and community landscapes.

Glossary

aeration: the process of introducing air into soil or water

Anthropocene: a term used to describe the geological era characterized by the significant and lasting impact of human activities on the Earth's geology and ecosystems

arthropod: a diverse and large group of invertebrate animals that includes insects and spiders

biennial plant: a type of flowering plant that completes its life cycle over the course of two years

biodiversity: the variety of life on Earth or in a particular ecosystem

biomass: the total mass of living organisms

brush pile: a collection or stack of small branches, twigs, and other woody debris that is intentionally arranged to create wildlife habitat

carbon sink: an area that absorbs more carbon from the atmosphere than it releases

climate change: the long-term alteration of Earth's average temperatures and weather patterns

community science: the involvement of the public, non-professional scientists or individuals from various backgrounds in scientific research, data collection, and analysis

companion planting: a gardening technique involving strategically planting compatible plants alongside each other, promoting natural pest control, improved pollination, enhanced nutrient uptake, and structural support

compost: a nutrient-rich, organic matter that results from the decomposition of various biodegradable materials, including kitchen scraps and yard waste

cultivar: short for cultivated variety, a plant variety that has been produced and maintained through intentional selection for specific traits

duff layer: the layer of decomposing organic material that accumulates on the forest floor

ecology: the study of the relationships between living organisms and their environments, including interactions between organisms and their physical surroundings, as well as the relationships among different species

ecoregion: a geographical area characterized by a distinct assemblage of ecosystems and ecological communities, often sharing similar environmental conditions and ecological features

ecosystem: a biological community of interacting organisms, including plants, animals, and microorganisms, and their physical environment

ecosystem services: the various benefits, including provisioning of resources, regulation of environmental processes, and support for life-sustaining functions, that ecosystems provide to humans and the broader environment

ectotherm: an organism that regulates its body temperature through environmental conditions, relying on external heat sources like sunlight

equity: having fairness in the distribution of resources, opportunities, and benefits that aim to address and rectify disparities that may exist among different individuals or groups

erosion: the process of the gradual wearing away or removal of soil, rock, or other materials from the Earth's surface, typically caused by water, wind, ice, or human activities

exotic plant: a plant not native to the continent on which it is now found

extinction: the complete and permanent disappearance of a species from the Earth

extirpation: the elimination of a species from a specific geographic area or habitat

food chain: the flow of energy from one trophic level to another as organisms feed on each other in an ecosystem

generalist species: an organism that can thrive in a wide range of environmental conditions and has a broad diet, allowing it to exploit a variety of resources

habitat: the specific environment where an organism or a community of organisms naturally resides and obtains the resources it needs to survive and reproduce

habitat fragmentation: the process by which a large, continuous habitat is broken into smaller, isolated patches or fragments

hardiness zone: a geographic area defined by a range of climatic conditions that are suitable for the survival and growth of particular types of plants

heat island effect: a phenomenon where urban areas experience higher temperatures compared to their surrounding rural areas

heirloom: a traditional, open-pollinated plant variety that has been passed down from one generation to another and is known for its genetic stability

herbicide: a type of pesticide specifically designed to control or eliminate the growth of unwanted plants

host plant: a plant species that serves as the habitat or source of nourishment for a particular organism

integrated pest management (IPM): a holistic and sustainable approach to managing pests that involves a blend of cultural, biological, and mechanical practices, along with the judicious application of pesticides only when absolutely necessary

invasive plant: a plant that is both non-native and able to establish on many sites, grow quickly, and spread to the point of disrupting plant communities or ecosystems

lasagna gardening: a method of creating no-till, no-dig garden beds by stacking compostable materials like cardboard, leaves, kitchen scraps, and newspaper to suffocate the grass

leaf litter: the layer of dead leaves and plant debris that accumulates on the forest floor or other natural environments with significant vegetation

light pollution: the excessive or misdirected artificial light produced by human activities that interferes with the natural darkness of the night sky

microclimate: the climate conditions that prevail in a specific, small-scale area, distinct from the surrounding larger region

migration: the regular, seasonal movement of a population of animals from one region to another

monoculture: the practice of cultivating a single crop species over a large area

mud kitchen: an outdoor play area where children can use their creativity and imagination to create bakery-inspired concoctions using water, soil, and other natural materials

mulch: a layer of material, such as leaves or wood chips, spread over the soil surface around plants to retain moisture, suppress weeds, regulate soil temperature, and enhance overall soil health

nativar: a cultivar of a native plant cultivated for specific traits like bloom color, size, or pest and disease resistance

native plant: a plant that is a part of the balance of nature that has developed over hundreds or thousands of years in a particular region or ecosystem

naturalized plant: a non-native plant that does not need human help to reproduce and maintain itself over time in an area where it is not native

No Mow May: an initiative that encourages homeowners and landowners to refrain from mowing their lawns during the month of May to promote the growth of floral resources that help bees and other pollinators

noise pollution: the excessive, disruptive, or harmful noise in the environment that interferes with normal activities, poses health risks, or disrupts the balance of ecosystems

non-native plant: a plant introduced with human help (intentionally or accidentally) to a new place or new type of habitat where it was not previously found

noxious weed: a plant that can directly or indirectly injure or cause damage to crops, livestock, or other interests of agriculture, irrigation, navigation, natural resources, public health, or the environment

ocean acidification: the ongoing decrease in the pH of the Earth's oceans, primarily caused by the absorption of carbon dioxide (CO_2) from the atmosphere

organic: a gardening method that avoids the use of synthetic pesticides, herbicides, fertilizers, and genetically modified organisms

ornamental plant: a landscape plant often grown for its aesthetic value such as showy leaves and flowers, foliage texture, or growth structure

ovipositor: the egg-laying organ in insects

parasite: an organism that lives on or in another organism, known as the host, and obtains nutrients and resources at the host's expense

parasitoid: an organism, typically an insect, that parasitizes another organism during its development, ultimately leading to the death of the host

peat bog: a type of wetland characterized by the accumulation of partially decayed organic matter, primarily peat

peat moss: a type of organic material that forms in waterlogged conditions where dead plant material accumulates without fully decomposing

perennial plant: a type of plant that lives for more than two years, typically producing flowers and seeds repeatedly throughout its life

pesticide: a chemical or substance designed to prevent, destroy, repel, or mitigate pests

photosynthesis: the biological process by which green plants, algae, and some bacteria convert light energy into chemical energy stored in the form of glucose or other sugars

plant blindness: a phenomenon that describes the human tendency to ignore plant species

plug: a small seedling or young plant that has been grown in a small container, usually in a greenhouse or nursery, before being transplanted into a larger growing space

pollination: the process by which pollen from the male reproductive organs (anthers) of a flower is transferred to the female reproductive organs (stigma) of the same or another flower, facilitating fertilization and the production of seeds and fruits

pollinator: an animal that plays a crucial role in the pollination process

predator: an animal that hunts and consumes other animals, known as prey

prey: an animal that is hunted and consumed by another animal known as a predator

primary producer: an organism or species that produces its own food through photosynthesis or chemosynthesis, forming the base of the food chain in an ecosystem

puddling station: a location where butterflies gather to engage in taking up nutrients from the soil

rain barrel: a container that collects rainwater from a rooftop and stores it for later use

rain chain: a series of linked cups, funnels, or other decorative elements that guide rainwater from the roof of a building to the ground

rain garden: a sunken garden bed that captures water from impervious surfaces and absorbs it into the ground before it reaches waterways

raised bed: a gardening technique that involves creating a planting area that is elevated above the surrounding ground level

runoff: the flow of water, usually from rainfall or snowmelt, over the surface of the land that occurs when there is more water than the land can naturally absorb

seed scarification: a horticultural technique that involves intentionally damaging or weakening the seed coat of certain hard-seeded plants to facilitate germination

seed stratification: a horticultural technique that involves subjecting seeds to a period of cold and moist conditions to simulate the natural winter conditions required for germination

seedling: a young, newly germinated plant

snag: a standing dead tree

soil pH: a measure of the acidity or alkalinity of soil

soil seed bank: the collection of seeds that are present in the soil

solarization: a process that uses heat from the sun to kill vegetation by covering it with clear plastic

specialist species: an organism with a narrow ecological niche, relying on specific habitat requirements, dietary preferences, and environmental tolerances

square-foot gardening: a gardening technique that involves dividing the garden into manageable square-foot sections, each dedicated to a specific crop

succession planting: the practice of carefully timing and coordinating multiple plantings to ensure a continuous harvest throughout your growing season

tilling: the practice of mechanically turning over and breaking up soil to prepare it for planting

topography: the physical features and characteristics of the Earth's surface, including elevation and slopes

transplant: a plant that has been uprooted and replanted

transverse orientation: the practice of keeping a fixed angle on a distant source of light to orient in the night sky

tree tube: a protective cylinder typically made of plastic or other materials that is placed around saplings or young trees to shield them from various environmental factors such as browsing by animals

turfgrass: a group of grass species that are commonly grown and managed as a groundcover in lawns, sports fields, golf courses, and other landscaped areas

urbanization: the process by which an increasing proportion of a population moves to urban areas, leading to the growth and expansion of cities and towns

vermicomposting: a composting method that uses specialized earthworms, such as red wigglers, to break down organic waste materials like kitchen scraps and plant matter

volatilization: the process by which a substance, usually a liquid or solid, is converted into a gas or vapor

watershed: an area of land that drains water from rainfall and snowmelt into small waterways, including creeks, streams, and tributaries

weed: a plant (native or non-native) that is not valued in the place where it is growing

wild-type or straight species: a native plant that is regionally specific and found naturally occurring in the wild without cultivation or hybridization

wind break: carefully planned rows of trees, shrubs, or other vegetation planted to shield a property from strong winds

window strike: an instance where a bird collides with a window or glass surface, often resulting in injury or mortality

Acknowledgments

First and foremost, I would like to thank my family. To my husband and children who put up with my excitement (and exhaustion) while I was writing and photographing this book, thank you. This was certainly a group project. To my dad who promised that if I found my passion, I'd never work a day in my life (you were wrong, but it certainly makes work more enjoyable). Thank you for always believing in me and helping me chase my dreams. And to my in-laws, David and Carol Wolfe, thank you for your critical review of content and your support along the way.

To all those who graciously invited me into your gardens to learn and to photograph and to those who helped procure photos: Elizabeth Anderson, Laura Burch, Brent Carr, Chelsea and Joseph Churpek, Ann Cicarella, Jeni Filburn, Susan Heady, Asya Palatova, Erin Parker, Becky Ramskogler, and Nate Yoder.

Finally, thank you to Timber Press and especially my editor, Ryan, who made my dreams come true by bringing this book into the world.

Photography and Illustration Credits

All photos are by the author except for the following:

Scott Wolfe, 8, 13 (top), 100, 120, 128, 130, 132

UNSPLASH
Erika Fletcher, 78 (left)
Max Gotts, 126 (bottom)

ILLUSTRATIONS
USDA, 17
USEPA, 18

References

Banks, J. L. and R. McConnell. 2015. "National Emissions from Lawn and Garden Equipment." *Proceedings of the 2015 International Emissions Inventory Conference*, San Diego, USA.

Frick, T. and D. Tallamy. 1996. "Density and Diversity of Nontarget Insects Killed by Suburban Electric Insect Traps." *Entomological News* 107 (2), 77–82.

Greenspoon, L., E. Krieger, R. Sender, Y. Rosenberg, Y. M. Bar-On, U. Moran, T. Antman, S. Meiri, U. Roll, & E. Noor. 2023. "The Global Biomass of Wild Mammals." *Proceedings of the National Academy of Sciences of the United States of America* 120 (10). doi.org/10.1073/pnas.2204892120.

Harris, N. L., D. A. Gibbs, A. Baccini, R. A. Birdsey, S. De Bruin, M. Farina, L. Fatoyinbo, M. C. Hansen, M. Herold, R. A. Houghton, P. Potapov, D. R. Suárez, R. M. Román-Cuesta, S. Saatchi, C. M. Slay, S. Turubanova, & A. Tyukavina. 2021. "Global Maps of Twenty-first Century Forest Carbon Fluxes." *Nature Climate Change* 11 (3), 234–240. doi.org/10.1038/s41558-020-00976-6.

Humphreys, A. M., R. Govaerts, S. Z. Ficinski, E. N. Lughadha, & M. S. Vorontsova. 2019. "Global Dataset Shows Geography and Life Form Predict Modern Plant Extinction and Rediscovery." *Nature Ecology and Evolution* 3 (7), 1043–1047. doi.org/10.1038/s41559-019-0906-2.

Kyba, C. C. M., Y.Ö. Altıntaş, C. E. Walker, & M. Newhouse. 2023. "Citizen Scientists Report Global Rapid Reductions in the Visibility of Stars from 2011 to 2022." *Science* 379 (6629), 265–268. doi.org/10.1126/science.abq7781.

Lerman, S. B., A. R. Contosta, J. Milam, & C. Bang. 2018. "To Mow or To Mow Less: Lawn Mowing Frequency Affects Bee Abundance and Diversity in Suburban Yards." *Biological Conservation* 221, 160–174. doi.org/10.1016/j.biocon.2018.01.025.

Loss, S. R., T. Will, & P. P. Marra. 2013. "The Impact of Free-ranging Domestic Cats on Wildlife of the United States." *Nature Communications* 4 (1). doi.org/10.1038/ncomms2380.

Milesi, C., S. W. Running, C. D. Elvidge, J. B. Dietz, B. T. Tuttle, & R. R. Nemani. 2005. "Mapping and Modeling the Biogeochemical Cycling of Turf Grasses in the United States." *Environmental Management* 36 (3), 426–438. doi.org/10.1007/s00267-004-0316-2.

Sánchez-Bayo, F., & K. A. G. Wyckhuys. 2019. "Worldwide Decline of the Entomofauna: A Review of its Drivers." *Biological Conservation* 232, 8–27. doi.org/10.1016/j.biocon.2019.01.020.

Stevenson, M., K. L. Hudman, A. Scott, K. Contreras, & J. G. Kopachena. 2021. "High Survivorship of First-Generation Monarch Butterfly Eggs to Third Instar Associated with a Diverse Arthropod Community." *Insects* 12 (6), 567. doi.org/10.3390/insects12060567.

Stothard, E. R., A. W. McHill, C. M. Depner, B. R. Birks, T. M. Moehlman, H. K. Ritchie, J. R. Guzzetti, E. D. Chinoy, M. K. LeBourgeois, J. Axelsson, & K. P. Wright. 2017. "Circadian Entrainment to the Natural Light-Dark Cycle across Seasons and the Weekend." *Current Biology* 27 (4), 508–513. doi.org/10.1016/j.cub.2016.12.041.

Tallamy, D. W. & K. J. Shropshire. 2009. "Ranking Lepidopteran Use of Native Versus Introduced Plants." *Conservation Biology* 23 (4), 941–947. doi.org/10.1111/j.1523-1739.2009.01202.x.

Index

About the Author

DENICE HAZLETT

Danae Wolfe is an award-winning conservation photographer, writer, educator, and TEDx speaker focused on fostering appreciation and stewardship of backyard bugs and wildlife. Ever the pragmatic, she believes that everyone has the power to make a difference in combatting climate change and biodiversity loss. Danae was the 2022 recipient of the Garden Communicators International Emergent Communicator award, and her work has been featured in various outlets including CNN, *The American Gardener* magazine, and *Nature Conservancy Magazine*. Through her community conservation initiative, Chasing Bugs, she has reached global audiences with science-based education about the importance of gardening for biodiversity and has inspired gardeners to appreciate the beauty of our natural world and embrace their role in its protection.